Terrorism and Global Security:
The Nuclear Threat

Other Titles in This Series

Terrorism: Theory and Practice, edited by Yonah Alexander, Paul Wilkinson, and David Carlton

Self-Determination: National, Regional, and Global Dimensions, edited by Yonah Alexander and Robert A. Friedlander

International Terrorism: An Annotated Bibliography and Research Guide, Augustus R. Norton and Martin H. Greenberg

Victims of Terrorism, edited by Frank M. Ochberg

Terrorism and Hostage Negotiations, Abraham H. Miller

Westview Special Studies in National and International Terrorism

Terrorism and Global Security: The Nuclear Threat
Louis René Beres

The enormous potential for destruction that lies latent in nuclear technology inevitably gives rise to the possibility of nuclear terrorism—the use of nuclear explosives or radioactivity by insurgent groups. Professor Beres considers the factors that might foster such terrorism, the forms it might take, and the probable consequences of each form. He then identifies a coherent strategy of counternuclear terrorism, one that embraces both technological and behavioral measures, that suggests policies for deterrence and situation management on both national and international levels, and that points toward a major refashioning of world order.

Louis René Beres, associate professor of political science at Purdue University, has lectured and published extensively on the subject of nuclear terrorism. His most recent books include *Planning Alternative World Futures: Values, Methods, and Models* and *Apocalypse: Nuclear Catastrophe in World Politics.*

//

Terrorism and Global Security:
The Nuclear Threat

Louis René Beres

Westview Press / Boulder, Colorado

*Westview Special Studies in National
and International Terrorism*

Copyright © 1979 by Westview Press, Inc.

Published in 1979 in the United States of America by
   Westview Press, Inc.
   5500 Central Avenue
   Boulder, Colorado 80301
   Frederick A. Praeger, Publisher

Library of Congress Cataloging in Publication Data
Beres, Louis René.
   Terrorism and global security.
   (Westview special studies in national and international terrorism)
   1. Terrorism. 2. Atomic power—International control. I. Title. II. Series.
HV6431.B47   301.6'33   79-16291
ISBN 0-89158-557-5

Printed and bound in the United States of America

For my parents
Sigmund and Margret Beres
Sine qua non

Contents

Preface

In the hazardous flux of world affairs, the specter of nuclear terrorism is particularly insidious. For the first time in humankind's history on this beleaguered planet, private *individuals* are capable of exploiting the destructive potential of nuclear technology. Understandably, fresh visions of oblivion and radioactive silence have kindled our apocalyptic imaginations, producing ever-greater levels of personal and collective insecurity. As if this were not frightful enough, those who might ultimately be confronted with responsibility for making crisis decisions concerning nuclear insurgency are frozen like the chorus in a Greek tragedy, distraught at the march of events that they feel powerless to control.

The situation *is* fraught with disquieting possibilities. But it is also too soon to despair. There are steps that can be taken, things that can and must be done, to prevent a new paradigm of violence. We need a plan, one that joins the elements of sound scholarship with the summoning and mastery of visions of atomic annihilation. With such a plan, we can begin to take the first critical steps back from a future that glows as a numbing hallucination.

The plan is complex. It cannot be limited to the sorts of "quick fix" physical security measures that are now in fashion. Rather, it must also include measures directed toward affecting the behavior of terrorists. And all strategies of counternuclear terrorism, technological and behavioral, need to be applied internationally.

Before we are able to finish our plan, we will understand its critical dependence upon a strengthened tapestry of international treaties and agreements directed at nonproliferation and superpower arms control. Moreover, because the success of counternuclear terrorism will require a major refashioning of the international legal order, we will explore the prospects for far-reaching transformations of foreign policy processes. In the final analysis, the prevention of nuclear terrorism will require states to move beyond the precarious dynamics of realpolitik to a new world politics of globalism. It would be futile to try to tinker with the portent of nuclear terrorism without such a change. *Planetization,* a new consciousness of unity and relatedness between states, is integral to all possibilities for enduring patterns of safety.

Let us begin our inquiry! After a conceptual examination of the terrorism phenomenon, we will consider the various factors that, in combination, might give rise to nuclear terrorism; the different forms that nuclear terrorism might take; and the probable consequences of each form. Thereafter, we will erect the scaffolding for a theory of counternuclear terrorism, a plan for deterrence and situation management that can inform promising policy efforts.

Lenin once observed, "Without a revolutionary theory, there is no revolutionary practice." The same relationship obtains between the theory of counternuclear terrorism and effective counternuclear terrorism in practice. Without the former, the latter is impossible. Recognizing this, we will construct a theory of counternuclear terrorism from which viable strategies, should they ever be needed, can be systematically derived.

I wish to thank the U.S. Arms Control and Disarmament Agency for supporting my earlier research on the subject of nuclear terrorism. Much of that research proved helpful in the preparation of this book. Of course, the views expressed in this book are those of the author, and do not necessarily represent the views of any other individual or agency of government.

L.R.B.

Part 1

Understanding Nuclear Terrorism

The Specter of Nuclear Terrorism:
An Overview

A Surrealist System: The Terrorist as Microcosm

The terrorist is a study in contradictions. He wishes the re-birth of a certain kind of order, but in the delivery a grave-digger must wield the forceps. He wishes to impress a world-wide public with the reasonableness of his claims, but chooses the tirade as his preferred means of communication. He stamps his predilections for violent excess with the imprimatur of innocence, yet it is only through the destruction of innocence that his aims can be realized.

How can we understand such contradictions? Even in the admittedly absurd theater of modern world politics, the terror-ist appears more than merely avant-garde. He appears genuinely pathological. Or is it, rather, the entire global human condition that is diseased, a disintegrating nonlandscape of irrationality in which only verbalized chaos remains truly comprehensible?

What is producing such contradictions? Is it an intangible but pervasive crisis of existential emptiness and despair from which human beings cannot escape? Is it the objectification of individuals into vast networks of social, economic, and politi-cal manipulation? Is it a fundamental disequilibrium that frac-tures the integrity of Earth's highly integrated system of cultural and biological adaptation?[1] Or is it "simply" the failure to satisfy the diverse political hopes of unhappy people in unbear-able circumstances?

Perhaps, in the Orwellian logic of our time, contradictions

must be redefined altogether. Why should they offend our sense of correct reason? After all, we live in a world where peace is sought through competition in strategic arms; where the legal equality of states coexists with an institutionalized hierarchy of authority in the United Nations; and where societies achieve high measures of growth through despoliation of their environment. It is a world wherein Watergate figures reap huge profits from accounts of their misdeeds; where convicted U.S. war criminals return to their pastoral hometowns as heroes; and where a former president of South Vietnam now runs a liquor store in California.

Against the backdrop of such a world, can the alleged contradictions of modern terrorism cause real consternation? Since George Orwell wrote the grim fantasy *1984,* his notion of doublethink has become a new orthodoxy of worldwide human relations. Understood as "the power of holding two contradictory beliefs in one's mind simultaneously, and accepting both of them," doublethink is now manifest not only in expressions of political propaganda, but also in the most widely revered documents of national and international law.

One such manifestation in the international legal order concerns the issue of effective counterterrorism. Although specially constituted UN committees have continually condemned acts of international terrorism in principle, they have exempted from the definition of such acts those activities that derive from "the inalienable right to self-determination and independence of all peoples under colonial and racist regimes and other forms of alien domination and the legitimacy of their struggle, in particular the struggle of national liberation movements, in accordance with the purposes and principles of the Charter and the relevant resolutions of the organs of the United Nations." This exemption, from the 1973 General Assembly *Report of the Ad Hoc Committee on International Terrorism*,[2] is corroborated by Article 7 of the General Assembly's 1974 *Definition of Aggression.* According to Article 7:

Nothing in this definition, and in particular Article 3 [inventory of acts that qualify as aggression[3]] could in any way prejudice the right to self-determination, freedom, and independence, as derived from the Charter, of peoples forcibly deprived of that right and referred to in the Declaration on Principles of International Law concerning Friendly Relations and Cooperation among States[4] in accordance with the Charter of the United Nations, particularly peoples under colonial and racist regimes or other forms of alien domination; nor the right of these peoples to struggle to that end and to seek and receive support, in accordance with the principles of the Charter and in conformity with the above-mentioned Declaration.[5]

Although such an exemption may be intended to protect the legitimacy of certain forms of insurgency, it has the same effect as earlier distinctions between just and unjust wars. That is, it offers a legal justification for virtually any acts of violence that can be cloaked in the appropriate juridical terms. To better understand the problem, we must first turn to its source—the individuals who practice the deeds that occasion this study.

Facing the Gorgon Head: The Nature of Modern Terrorism

Today's terrorists are spurred on by a variety of motives. Some are moved by the wish to alter the devastating inequities of an unjust order. Here, there exists a long and venerable tradition. Where it is understood as resistance to despotism, terrorism has been countenanced and supported in the Bible and in the writings of ancient and medieval classics. The tyrannicide motif can be found in Aristotle's *Politics*, Plutarch's *Lives*, and Cicero's *De Officiis*. According to Cicero:

There can be no such thing as fellowship with tyrants, nothing but bitter feud is possible: and it is not repugnant to nature to despoil, if you can, those whom it is a virtue to kill; nay, this pestilent and godless brood should be utterly banished from human society. For, as we amputate a limb in which the blood and the vital spirit have ceased to circulate, because it injures the rest of the body, so monsters, who, under human guise, conceal the cruelty and ferocity of a wild beast, should be severed from the common body of humanity.[6]

Other terrorists, in the fashion of bandits, are moved by the selfish search for material gain. Still others, like the protagonist of André Malraux's *The Human Condition,* base their motive, consciously or unconsciously, on the need to escape from one form or another of private anguish. In this last category, we discover the "incapacity for authentic relatedness" described in the various writings of Erich Fromm, the *emptiness* of T. S. Eliot's "hollow men," and the *bottomless rage* that is brought on by repeated and unrelenting doses of misfortune, a rage that produces the kinds of effects asserted by Shakespeare's Second Murderer in Act 2, Scene 1 of *Macbeth*:

> I am one, my liege,
> Whom the vile blows and buffets of the world,
> Hath so incensed, that I am reckless what
> I do to spite the world.

Occasionally, this combination of traits foments a genuinely psychopathic breed of terrorist, one who says, with Jerry Rubin, "When in doubt, burn," or one who feels, with Kozo Okamoto, the surviving terrorist of the Lydda Airport massacre, "a strange ecstasy" in meting out death to innocents. Here, we are faced with the values of a Nechaev, the nineteenth-century Russian terrorist who served as one of the models for Dostoevski's major figure in *The Possessed*:

> He (the revolutionary) knows of only one science, the science of destruction. To this end, and this end alone, he will study mechanics, physics, chemistry, and perhaps medicine. To this end he will study day and night the living science: people, their characters and circumstances and all the features of the present social order at all possible levels. His sole and constant object is the immediate destruction of this vile order.[7]

One modern terrorist who has explicitly identified himself with this "revolutionary catechism" is Renato Curcio, founder of the Italian Red Brigades. In his writings, Curcio cites approvingly from Nechaev:

> The revolutionary has neither personal business nor sentimental interests. He is without ties, property, or even a name. In the depth of his being, not only in words but in deeds, he has ruptured every tie with civil order and with all of the civilized world—with law, with custom, with morality, and those conventions generally recognized as of this world.[8]

In certain cases, today's terrorists bear a bizarre resemblance to punk rockers, whose dominant rationale is to move, to shock, to goad, to outrage, to reveal potency without any real underlying ideology. For punk rockers, the essential tools of the trade are guitar, bass, and drums amplified to a neurologically destructive volume. For psychopathic terrorists, the essential implements are the instruments of violence, readied for indiscriminate slaughter.

Should such terrorists ever acquire the instruments of nuclear violence, the results may well include an unprecedented spasm of gratuitous killing and maiming. It would surely be a major mistake to conclude that such terrorists are incapable of wreaking profound unhappiness because of their condition. As Freud points out:

> Fools, visionaries, sufferers from delusions, neurotics, and lunatics have played great roles at all times in the history of mankind, and not merely when the accident of birth had bequeathed them sovereignty. Usually, they have wreaked havoc.

But we must not assume that only psychopathic terrorists are captivated by the romanticization of excessive violence. Adhering closely to Frantz Fanon's words in *The Wretched of the Earth*, Al Fatah has articulated a doctrine of "liberation" through cataclysmic violence. Although such liberation is cast in terms of its unifying and purgative effects, it is also directed at a clear set of political/historical objectives.[9]

Origins and Regularities

Terrorism is not a recent phenomenon. It is older than the ancient civilizations of Greece and Rome. Early examples include the assassination of Julius Caesar in 44 B.C.; the examples of the *Sicarii,* a religious sect, during the first century A.D. Zealot struggle in Palestine; and the acts of secret Islamic armed bands in the twelfth and thirteenth centuries. Contemporary scholars, however, tend to focus upon much later origins, namely the methods of Robespierre, Saint-Just, and Couthon during the French Reign of Terror (1793-1794). Perhaps the single most astounding fact about these terrorists is that their accusations, coming from the Committee of Public Safety, led a nation of 27 million people into sending as many as 40,000 to the guillotine and 300,000 to jail. All told, Robespierre and his band probably numbered no more than twenty-two.[10]

How is it that such a small group could wield such enormous power? The answer, of course, is *fear.* By manipulating fear in a special way, the terrorists were able to affect political behavior in a fashion totally disproportionate to their numbers.

In the political realm, fear produces intimidation when it issues from the threat of violence. It is not necessary to modify this statement by speaking exclusively of arbitrary or indiscriminate violence, since these characteristics are an irremediable part of the definition. All violence, as Hannah Arendt reminds us, is unpredictable.[11]

Unlike power, force, or strength, violence is always applied with unforseeable effects. The ensuing domination by *Fortuna,* or fate, creates a devastating aura of uncertainty, one in which the hegemony of means over ends paralyzes the will of potential opponents. As a result, terrorism is consecrated as an "improvement" upon war as the *ultima ratio* in world affairs, a strategy whereby the *weak* become effectual participants on the global stage.

Since the close of the eighteenth century, we have had a great many instances of terrorism. Historically, we may point to the struggle that led to the Irish Treaty of 1921; the tactics of the *Irgun Zvai Leumi* in Palestine; the postwar movements for national liberation in Algeria and Kenya; and the diverse array of current activities throughout the world, including even North America. During World War II, terrorism took place as an adjunct to conventional warfare, occasioning many people to question the reasonableness of a blanket condemnation of a strategy that clearly had its place under certain conditions. After all, many who found it difficult to accept other forms of insurgency could not quarrel with partisan or resistance efforts directed at brutal foreign oppressors.

In view of this astounding heterogeneity, are there any ascertainable *regularities*, common features concerning characteristics and composition that are essential to theorizing about terrorism? Looking over the current landscape of operational groups, we find anarchists, separatists, Marxist-Leninists, black nationalists, new left activists, right wing reactionaries, Castroites, Trotskyists, and every conceivable brand of anti-imperialist and national liberationist.[12] Their intellectual and spiritual mentors include a gallery of heroes featuring Bakhunin, Marx, Lenin, Trotsky,[13] Sorel, Marighella, Mao, Giap, Fanon, Marcuse, Malcolm X, Guevara, Debray, and Guillen. What could this tangled skein of programs and participants possibly have in common?

This question appears even more problematic when one considers the fragmentation and factionalization within particular groups and movements. For example, the Irish Republican Army (IRA) has been split since 1969 into an "official" faction, which exhibits a Marxist-Leninist orientation, and a "provisional" faction, which aims at unification of Ireland. The situation among the Palestinian groups is Byzantine in its complexity. Subsumed under a loose umbrella of the Palestine Liberation Organization (PLO) are Al Fatah, which is nationalist and non-Marxist; Black September, the principal terrorist arm of Al Fatah; the Popular Front for the Liberation of Palestine (PFLP), which is dominated by the Marxist-Leninist Arab National Movement of George Habash; the Popular Front for the Liberation of Palestine—General Command (PFLP—GC), which formed as a splinter from the PFLP in 1970 because of major disagreements; and the Popular Democratic Front for the Liberation of Palestine (PDFLP), which is Maoist in ideology.

Nonetheless, these strange bedfellows have identified enough commonality to cooperate across geographic and ideological lines. The IRA Provisionals have established links with the PFLP. The Red Army Faction of West Germany, sometimes known as the Baader-Meinhof Group, is believed to have extensive ties to the Japanese Red Army Group and to various Palestinian terrorist organizations. The Red Army (*Rengo Sekigun*) operates in Western Europe in alignment with Palestinian groups as well as with the Red Army Faction. Outside of Europe, it is also known to coordinate operations with the Uruguayan *Tupamaros*.[14] The so-called Carlos Group, named after the alias of leader Illich Ramirez-Sanchez, has worked closely with various Palestinian groups, the Red Army, and the Baader-Meinhof Group.[15]

What do these cooperative terrorist ventures suggest? A single "terrorist mind" which, if properly understood, will produce effective strategies of counterterrorism? By no means! But there have been some attempts to create a "profile of terrorists." Such attempts do not contradict the fundamental heterogeneity of the subject, but they do illuminate some interesting (if not really useful) commonalities.

Perhaps the best of these attempts is the study by Charles A. Russell and Bowman H. Miller, "Profile of a Terrorist," which appeared in the academic journal, *Terrorism*.[16] Using data predominantly from foreign news sources, the authors stipulate a general sociological profile of today's terrorist. Their composite is revealed as "a single male, aged 22 to 24, with at least a partial university education, most often in the humanities." Moreover, the prototype terrorist seems to prefer a career in law, medicine, journalism, or teaching, although in Turkish and Iranian groups, engineering and technical occupations have also been favored. With respect to social origins, "Today's terrorist comes from an affluent middle- or upper-class family that enjoys some social prestige."[17]

While such profiles are admittedly intriguing, they do not significantly advance the search for essential theory. After all, the identification of common characteristics regarding age, sex, marital status, rural versus urban origin, social and economic background, education or occupation, method or place of recruitment, and political-economic philosophy (the organizing dimensions of the Russell-Miller study) does not lead to the sort of behavioral strategy that can reduce the likelihood of nuclear terrorism. To create such a strategy we need to ask different questions, ones that explore far more crucial variables than those selected by the profilers.

What kinds of questions are these? They are questions that are intended to produce a fuller understanding of the risk calculations of terrorists. Hence, they focus upon those variables that are most likely to affect such calculations. Until we understand the special terrorist stance on the balance of risks that can be taken in world politics, and the vital differences between terrorist groups on this stance, we will not be able to identify an appropriate system of sanctions.

To properly understand the decisional calculi of terrorist groups, therefore, we must first come to grips with the following questions. This will be done throughout the remainder of this study.

1. Is there a particular ordering of preferences that is common to many or all terrorist groups, or is there significant variation from one group to another? If it can be determined that many or all terrorist groups actually share a basic hierarchy of wants, a general strategy of counternuclear terrorist operations can begin to be shaped. Alternatively, if significant variation in preference orderings can be detected between terrorist groups, myriad strategies of an individually "tailored" nature will have to be identified.

2. Are there particular preferences that tend to occupy the highest positions in the preference hierarchies of terrorist groups, and how might these preferences be effectively obstructed? In this connection, it is especially important to examine the widely held assumption that terrorists, like states, are most anxious to avoid negative physical sanctions. In fact, a great deal of sophisticated conceptual analysis and experimental evidence appears to indicate that such sanctions are apt to be ineffective in limiting aggression and may actually prove counterproductive.

3. To what extent, if any, would the obstruction of terrorist preferences prove offensive to some of the principal values of states? In this case, we must be concerned about the very real possibility that effective counternuclear terrorist measures might be injurious to such values as social justice and human rights within particular states. Here, states must first decide whether the prospective benefits of proposed antiterrorist activity are great enough to outweigh the prospective costs to major segments of their own populations.

4. To what extent, if any, are the risk calculations of terrorist actors affected by geographic dispersion and intermingling with state actors? Since terrorists do not occupy a piece of territory in the manner of states, they are not susceptible to orthodox threats of deterrence. How, then, might effective counternuclear terrorist efforts be reconciled with the reality of geographic dispersion?

5. To what extent, if any, might the decisional calculi of terrorist actors be receptive to positive cues or sanctions as opposed to negative ones, and exactly what rewards seem to warrant consideration? In this connection, special attention might be directed to studies of child rearing, which indicate with overwhelming regularity that positive sanctions (rewards) are generally far more effective than negative ones (punishment).

6. To what extent would the implementation of effective counternuclear terrorist measures require special patterns of

international cooperation, and how might such patterns be created? In principle, the surest path to success in averting nuclear terrorism lies in a unified opposition to terrorist activity by states; yet, at least in the immediate future, this kind of opposition is assuredly not forthcoming. We must, therefore, ask ourselves what cooperative patterns between *particular* states can cope with the problem under discussion.

7. To what extent, if any, are the risk calculations of terrorists affected by their relations with "host" states? Since terrorist actors necessarily operate within the framework of individual states, the character of the relationship between "visitor" and "host" may affect the viability of counternuclear terrorist measures. How, therefore, might we exploit what is known about such relationships in curbing the threat of nuclear terrorism?

8. To what extent, if any, are the risk calculations of terrorist actors affected by alignments with state actors or with other terrorist groups? And how, therefore, can we use what we know about such effects to devise an effective counternuclear terrorist strategy?

9. To what extent, if any, are the risk calculations of terrorist actors affected by the terrorist pattern of random and uninhibited violence? In asking this particular question, we treat terrorist orientations to violence as an independent variable in order to treat it more effectively as a dependent variable later on.

10. To what extent, if any, are the risk calculations of terrorist actors affected by the degree to which their policies evoke sympathy and support from others? Since almost all acts of terror are essentially propagandistic, it is important to understand their desired effects on selected publics in order to prevent escalation to a nuclear option.

By considering these basic questions, students of nuclear terrorism can create the foundations of a genuinely auspicious behavioral strategy. With such a strategy in hand, steps can be taken to create inhibitions in the use of violence by terrorists and to impede the growing cooperation of terrorist groups. As with all other groups of human beings, terrorists acquire a repertoire of behavior under the particular contingencies of reinforcement to which they are exposed. The "trick" is to understand this repertoire and to use it to inform the differential reinforcement of alternative courses of action. Once this is done, the specter of nuclear terrorism can be confronted with countermeasures that are grounded in a coherent "profile" of variables likely to affect terrorist actions. Such a profile, rather than an inventory of extraneous commonalities concerning age, sex, marital status, etc., is logically antecedent to successful strategies of deterrence and situation management.

The Etiology of Nuclear Terrorism: Five Harbingers

It is now widely understood that terrorist access to weapons of mass destruction represents the single most substantial portent of nuclear terrorism.[1] However, such access assumes serious dimensions only when it is coupled with four additional conditions: terrorist orientations to nuclear violence; terrorist insensitivity to traditional threats of deterrence; cooperation between terrorist groups; and tolerance and support of terrorism. In this chapter, we will explore these five factors, which—taken together—give rise to an unprecedented hazard.

Terrorist Access to Nuclear Weapons

In a century wherein man has learned to stoke the crematory fires with enthusiasm, nothing can give greater cause for alarm than the access of terrorists to nuclear weapons, nuclear power plants, or nuclear waste storage facilities. Yet, there is now considerable evidence that suggests that determined terrorist groups might acquire nuclear weapons via the theft of assembled systems from military stockpiles or by self-development from pilfered weapons-grade nuclear material. It is also widely recognized that terrorists might attempt to sabotage nuclear reactors.

To acquire an assembled weapon, terrorist operatives might aim at any of the tens of thousands of nuclear weapons now deployed in the national arsenals of the United States, the

Soviet Union, France, England, and China. Such terrorists are likely to have an enlarged arena of opportunity in the future. This is because the number of states possessing nuclear weapons is growing steadily and because new members of the nuclear club are apt to waive essential safeguards.

This does not mean, however, that existing U.S. safeguards are satisfactory.[2] Reporting on an April 1974 fact-finding trip to U.S. Air Force NATO nuclear weapons installations in Turkey, columnist Bob Wiedrich wrote of nuclear weapons as "potentially ripe for the plucking by any band of terrorists dedicated enough to risk their own lives." Quoting the Air Force officer in charge of his briefing, Wiedrich wrote, "Any force of heavily armed terrorists could conceivably mount a successful attack to steal one of the weapons." The deep concern voiced by that U.S. officer is still widely shared by responsible students of nuclear terrorism.[3]

Among these students are members of Congress, who looked into the security of U.S. nuclear weapons overseas during the period 1973-1975[4] and who have reexamined the issue during 1978 as part of an overall counterterrorist effort.[5] According to Senator John Glenn, speaking during hearings before the Senate Committee on Governmental Affairs concerning prospective antiterrorist legislation:

> I would submit, as far as terrorism goes, that we haven't reached the worst stage yet. We have spread thousands upon thousands of artillery shells of nuclear capability around the world. We have increasing capability to miniaturize these weapons. Some day, one or more of them will turn up missing. Someone will be able to carry them in a backpack.[6]

The Department of Defense (DOD) is continually working on ways to improve the protection of nuclear-weapon sites. In the wake of the terrorist attack at the 1972 Olympic Games, the DOD initiated a specific site security upgrade program. This program, which will cost between $330 and $340 million, is scheduled for completion by 1980, and will emphasize greater hardening of storage facilities, improved lighting, and more stringent standards for reaction forces.[7]

Moreover, the Department of Defense maintains task forces for counterterrorist emergencies. These forces have been approved by the Joint Chiefs of Staff for missions calling for the recovery/neutralization/destruction of stolen nuclear weapons.[8] The present configuration of U.S. military forces with counterterrorist capabilities includes U.S. Army Ranger Battalions; U.S. Marine Corps Battalion Landing Teams; USMC Marine Amphibious Unit; U.S. Army Special Forces; U.S. Marine Force Reconnaissance Company; U.S. Navy Sea, Air, Land (SEAL) Platoons; and Air Force support.[9]

Yet, the threat persists. There have been several incidents related to possible theft attempts directed at American nuclear-weapon storage sites in Europe.[10] Although DOD protection of assembled nuclear weapons is allegedly on a higher order of effectiveness than Department of Energy (DOE) and Nuclear Regulatory Commission (NRC) protection of strategic special nuclear materials,[11] it has been acknowledged that private individuals may have access to blueprints and electrical wiring diagrams for protective guard stations at nuclear facilities.[12] In apparent compliance with freedom of information requirements, the DOD has reportedly passed out, as public literature upon request, such specific information about nuclear storage areas as character and location of metal detectors, special nuclear material detectors, door controls, and explosive detectors.[13] According to Senator John Glenn, who discussed and revealed this information in hearings before the Senate Committee on Governmental Affairs on March 23, 1978:

> These particular diagrams here are not only electrical plans, they go into architectural details concerning where those plans fit in, structural plans and details, the actual construction diagrams here; another one, back to the Air Force base again (in earlier remarks, Senator Glenn had discussed the compromise of security at an air base undergoing security improvements) weapons storage area, entry control facilities, plans and specifics showing all the details

of it, all the wiring diagrams; another wiring diagram in detail here, and actual architectural layouts of where the wiring goes with regard to fencing and fence gate controls. There are details on the alarm hookup, with certain types of wiring, and even where they go and actually plotted on these charts as to where they are within the specific buildings.[14]

In view of such revelations, it would appear that DOD's nuclear security upgrade measures are impaired by DOD's indiscriminate passing out of security information. However, as indicated in testimony to Senator Glenn by Thomas J. O'Brien, director for security plans and programs, Department of Defense, a great deal of this information is open to the public under the Freedom of Information Act. Furthermore, according to O'Brien, such information would be of considerable help to a nuclear terrorist seeking entry into a nuclear storage area.[15]

Self-Development of Nuclear Weapons

To manufacture their own nuclear weapons, terrorists would require both strategic special nuclear materials and the expertise to convert them into a bomb or radiological weapon. As is now widely revealed, both requirements are well within the range of terrorist capabilities.[16] Consider the following information:

First, from a recent report to the Nuclear Regulatory Commission:

There is no doubt that terrorism is becoming an increasingly important weapon in the arsenal of those who wish to force their demands upon society. . . . A terrorist group would have few means more effective to threaten the lives of innocent people than the theft of SSNM (Strategic Special Nuclear Materials). Thus, the possibility of theft or diversion of SSNM must be considered one of the most serious potential dangers to society, especially if the material is used to construct and threaten detonation of a nuclear device.[17]

Second, from a recent statement by the Union of Concerned Scientists:

Present safeguards are inadequate to prevent plutonium (a by-product of commercial reactors that can be used in making atomic bombs) from being hijacked by terrorists or others who wish to sabotage or blackmail the United States government.[18]

Third, from recent testimony before a Senate committee by Dr. Theodore B. Taylor, a distinguished nuclear weapons engineer:

My view of the physical security safeguards of material that is not under the control of the Department of Defense or of the Department of Energy in the context of the nuclear weapons program is that it is still inadequate. What I mean by that is that the published regulations of the Nuclear Regulatory Commission, in my view, if abided by to the letter, and even somewhat beyond the letter, would not prevent groups of people with the types of skills and resources and motivation that have been used in successful attempts at theft in the past of other values. There have been I think important improvements of the physical security situation during the last dozen years or so. However, in the civilian facilities, certainly those under civilian control, I think it is still fair to say that the places where enough highly enriched uranium or plutonium to make at least one bomb exists, the physical security is not as good as it is in many financial institutions now for protecting money.[19]

And fourth, the disturbingly corroborative testimony of NRC Commissioner Victor Gilinsky, responding to inquiries from Senator Glenn concerning requirements for NRC licensees:

Senator Glenn. What does NRC do in that regard, Mr. Gilinsky?

Mr. Gilinsky. There are no specific clearance requirements for the licensees. Now most of the material . . .

Senator Glenn. Wait a minute. Say that again? There are no clearance requirements for licensees?

Mr. Gilinsky. At the present time, yes. Now we have published a proposed rule in March 1978 and we are scheduling hearings in

May or June on a rule which would require clearance of employees with access or control over this . . .

Senator Glenn. Are employees now operating NRC monitored plants—certainly there is some security classification they must run through, is there not? Is there no requirement for people licensed by you to have some sort of security clearance at all?

Mr. Gilinsky. There is not. Let me just qualify that. Most of the material handled is defense related. The contractor requires employees to have "Q" clearances. Let me put it this way: Essentially most of the employees that are in fact in this category have clearances, but there is no specific NRC requirement. There are some employees handling it in the private sector who do not have clearances.

Senator Glenn. There would be employees right now that are outside the DOD control that would be working at these facilities and have access to special nuclear material who have no classification; is that correct, or have not passed any security clearance?

Mr. Gilinsky. I believe that is right, yes.

Senator Glenn. I can't believe that has gone this long without somebody doing something about that. That is incredible to me. These people would have access, have potential access to special nuclear material.

Mr. Gilinsky. Yes, sir.

Senator Glenn. To either plutonium or highly enriched uranium.

Mr. Gilinsky. Yes.[20]

The problem of inadequate safeguards for special nuclear materials is highlighted by actual incidents involving loss or diversion. In August 1977, several members of both houses of Congress called for investigations following the release of a government report that indicates that nuclear fuel plants cannot account for *thousands of pounds* of special nuclear materials (a nuclear weapon can be fabricated with an amount of plutonium on the order of kilograms). Although the report stresses that there is no evidence of theft, the government has been unable to account for more than 8,000 pounds of uranium and plutonium that have disappeared since World War II.[21]

According to a series of documents released on August 22, 1977, by the Energy Research and Development Administration (ERDA), there have been very serious problems in the way in which U.S. authorities have kept track of bomb-grade nuclear materials in the hands of private companies. Among other things, the documents reveal that one U.S. company with close ties to two foreign governments reported that it had "lost" enough uranium to make at least ten nuclear weapons. The "gap" in the nation's accounting system was tied to the absence of procedures to detect a U.S. company that shipped more than a contracted amount of nuclear material out of the country in "collusion with a foreign customer."[22]

In February 1978, a special investigation by the Nuclear Regulatory Commission concluded that "its top staff official misled Congress in saying the Commission had no evidence that atomic materials had ever been stolen." While denying a deliberate deception, the investigation found that this official had "testified incorrectly" during the summer of 1977 when he agreed with a statement that members of the NRC "believe that no significant quantities of special nuclear materials have ever been diverted or stolen." The NRC investigation focused special attention on the still-mysterious disappearance of a large amount of highly enriched uranium from a nuclear facility in Apollo, Pennsylvania, in the mid-1960s.[23]

More than one year later, in March 1978, NRC Commissioner Gilinsky presented further evidence on missing plutonium. Explaining that the accounting system for strategic special nuclear materials is still in a "relatively rudimentary stage," Mr. Gilinsky conceded that "we simply don't have the technology that can really keep track of the material on a current basis." Adding to this information, Dr. Donald M. Kerr, acting assistant secretary for defense programs, Department of Energy, admitted that "we cannot prove to you that there was no diversion (of SSNM) in the Apollo incident."[24]

But not all cases of missing nuclear materials are cloaked in uncertainty. A significant number of cases in which diversion has been confirmed was documented by the Nuclear Regulatory Commission, Office of Nuclear Material Safety and Safeguards, Division of Safeguards. On April 27, 1978, in response to Senator Glenn's inquiry to NRC Commissioner Gilinsky of March 23, 1978, Carlton Kammerer, NRC's director of congressional affairs, sent Senator Glenn a list of incidents or threats known to the NRC that concern nuclear facilities. This "Safeguards Summary Event List" contains nine categories of events involving NRC licensed material or licensees. Category 3, entitled *Missing and/or Allegedly Stolen,* includes eighty-four entries. Category 4, entitled *Transportation,* includes thirty-one entries. According to the NRC, *"Transportation* related events include any occurrence where licensed material was misrouted, threatened, or reported missing or stolen during transport."[25]

All of these insights into the deficiencies of U.S. safeguards are disturbing. Yet, it is even more disturbing to recognize that the removal of these deficiencies might have no significant effect upon the prospect of nuclear-materials theft. This is the case because the protection of strategic special nuclear materials must be effective on a worldwide basis. U.S. safeguards cannot secure us against nuclear weapons fashioned from nuclear materials stolen elsewhere.

Regrettably, the amount of nuclear materials present in other countries is certain to expand at an alarming rate. The current international deals involving pilot reprocessing plants to extract weapons-grade plutonium from spent reactor-fuel rods signal dangerous conditions. Unless immediate and effective steps are taken to inhibit the spread of plutonium reprocessing and uranium enrichment facilities to other countries, terrorist opportunities to acquire fissionable materials for nuclear weapons purposes will reach very high limits.

To manufacture its own nuclear weapons, a terrorist group would also require expertise. It is now well known that such expertise is widely available. In 1977, the Office of Technology Assessment (OTA) produced a report entitled *Nuclear Proliferation and Safeguards.* After a general description of the two basic methods of assembling fissile material in a nuclear explosive (i.e., the assembly of two or more subcritical masses using gun propellants and the achievement of supercriticality of fissile material via high explosive), the report stated that "Militarily useful weapons with reliable nuclear yields in the kiloton range can be constructed with reactor-grade plutonium, using low technology." Moreover, "Given the weapons material and a fraction of a million dollars, a small group of people, none of whom had ever had access to the classified literature, could possibly design and build a crude nuclear explosive device."[26]

Approximately three years before the OTA report, a book by Mason Willrich and Theodore Taylor first opened the eyes of policy makers and informed citizens. According to the authors, "The design and manufacture of a crude nuclear explosive is no longer a difficult task technically, and a plutonium dispersal device which can cause widespread radioactive contamination is much simpler to make than an explosive."[27] On March 22, 1978, in a statement presented to the Senate Committee on Governmental Affairs, Dr. Taylor elaborated on his views:

Given the required amounts of special nuclear materials (plutonium, highly enriched uranium, uranium-233, or any other heavy elements from which fission explosives can be made without having to perform isotope enrichment), in a variety of chemical and physical forms, it is highly credible that a small group of people could design and build fission explosives, using information and non-nuclear materials that are accessible to the public worldwide. Under some circumstances, it is quite conceivable that this could be done by one person, working alone. Such explosives could be transported by automobile. Their probable explosive yields would depend considerably on the knowledge and skills of the group. Relatively crude explosives that would be likely to yield the equivalent of up to about 1000 tons of high explosive would be much easier to build than explosives that could be reliably expected to yield the equivalent of more than 10 kilotons of high explosive. Explosives with yields in the latter range would be much easier to build with highly enriched uranium or uranium-233 than with plutonium. All three materials, including plutonium of all isotopic compositions, could be used for making relatively crude explosives with yields in the vicinity of one kiloton.[28]

For several years, Dr. Taylor's views concerning terrorist fabrication of nuclear explosives have been challenged by others. In most cases, Dr. Taylor's acquaintance with classified information made it impossible to respond to these challenges satisfactorily. However, on March 15, 1978, he was shown a draft manuscript on the design and manufacture of nuclear weapons written by Dimitri Rotow, an undergraduate student. This manuscript, entitled "Nuclear Weapons Design and Construction," was written without expert assistance of any kind and without access to classified national security information or restricted data. Commenting on these efforts of a twenty-two-year-old student, Dr. Taylor testified:

> Mr. Rotow's manuscript is the most extensive and detailed exposition that I have seen outside the classified literature. Although it contains a number of errors, these do not generally detract from his main lines of reasoning in setting down a variety of approaches to the design of a variety of types of fission weapons. I was astonished by the amount of well-organized information and the number and quality of ideas he was able to assemble in a time that he says was about three months of intensive work. I would say his exposition is much stronger in dealing with design principles, and the reasoning behind them, than on estimates of performance, in which I found significant errors. All in all, however, I was neither shocked nor surprised that an intelligent and innovative person without extensive training in nuclear physics could produce such a document, though I was surprised that it took so little time. His work certainly tends to confirm a conviction I have held for more than 12 years.[29]

Mr. Rotow's work was not the first to underscore the credibility of the Taylor argument. That distinction belongs to a twenty-year-old Massachusetts Institute of Technology undergraduate who created an accurate technical design for a fission explosive that was documented in the "Nova" science series on public television on March 9, 1975. Later, a much more widely publicized case involved a twenty-one-year old physics major at Princeton University, who designed an atomic bomb in four months with information obtained entirely from public documents. The point of his design, said John Aristotle Phillips, who has since written a best-selling book on the affair, "was to show that any undergraduate with a physics background can do it, and therefore that it is reasonable to assume that terrorists could do it too."[30]

Less widely recognized, but similarly worth considering, are the cases of two small U.S. journals that have printed articles on building atomic bombs, and the "bomb class" at a student-run experimental college. Articles in both the underground newspaper, *Take Over,* and the feminist journal, *Majority Report,* contained detailed plans on how to build an atomic bomb using a coffee can and explosives. The article in *Take Over,* which was published in the July 4, 1974 issue, was adapted by the feminist journal with the title, "Handy Woman's Guide: How to Build Your Own Atomic Bomb and Strike a Balance of Power with the Patriarchy."[31]

A course entitled "How to Build an Atomic Bomb" was introduced at the University of Connecticut's Experimental College in the fall 1977 semester. Its purpose, according to the college's handbook, is "to draw attention to the dangers of nuclear power." By demonstrating the "comparative ease with which an atomic bomb can be made," the course hoped to demonstrate the dangers of nuclear terrorism.[32]

All of the foregoing cases involve *fission* explosives. The clandestine manufacture of a pure *fusion* explosive (a device that would not require any fission "trigger" to initiate explosive thermonuclear reactions in very light hydrogen isotopes such as deuterium and tritium) is another matter entirely. Such explosives require very sophisticated equipment, exceptionally skilled and experienced experts, and large sums of money.

With these facts in mind, the case involving *Progressive*

magazine's blocked attempt to publish an article entitled "How a Hydrogen Bomb Works" can be viewed in a more rational perspective. This case, which broke to the public in March 1979, concerns an article written by a thirty-six-year-old free-lance writer with little scientific experience. Moreover, the article was written without the benefit of classified materials. Apart from the esoteric questions of constitutionality that are involved in this matter, it is exceedingly unlikely that such an article would benefit aspiring nuclear terrorists. Indeed, the extraordinary difficulties that would be entailed in *fusion* terrorism have been identified by Mr. Rotow in Senate testimony:

> I think it is highly unlikely that any terrorist group would ever have the technical sophistication to actually produce a thermonuclear device. I have made several runthroughs at designing thermonuclear triggers and discovered that, in my understanding of the particular configuration the Government used to produce efficient triggers to detonate a thermonuclear device, it is a rather difficult thing to do, both to calculate it out and to actually build it. Building the thermonuclear part of the bomb, in any event, would involve terrorists diverting quantities of tritium and several other exotic isotopes of hydrogen and lithium. So I don't think that is rather likely, although I feel absolutely certain that a team of two physicists or perhaps even a single physicist, a nuclear engineer, could go through the existing literature in a period of less than 6 months and by reviewing all of the data on fusion research or power plant design come up with quite an accurate and convincing design for thermonuclear weapons. There is the concern that such a device would cost an incredible amount to build. My first try at such a design resulted in something that would easily cost several million dollars and would be about the size of a railroad tank car.[33]

Sabotage of Nuclear Reactors

Another path to nuclear capability by terrorists might involve the sabotage of nuclear reactor facilities. With images of the Three Mile Island accident and "The China Syndrome" fresh in our minds, it is apparent that such acts could pose monumental problems for responsible government authorities. Although a great many steps appear to have been taken in the United States during the past few years to diminish the vulnerability of nuclear power plants,[34] sabotage is certainly conceivable. Consider the following views of nuclear plant sabotage:

Testifying before the Joint Committee on Atomic Energy in March 1974, a former U.S. Navy underwater demolitions officer stated that any three to five underwater demolition or Green Beret officers could "sabotage virtually any nuclear reactor in the country."[35] Later in that same year, after improved security regulations had been implemented, the General Accounting Office stated, "Licensee and AEC officials agreed that a security system at a licensed nuclear plant could not prevent a takeover for sabotage by a small number—as few perhaps as two or three armed individuals."[36] A recent study prepared by the Sandia Corporation concludes, "It appears that a sufficiently determined and able group could perform acts of sabotage which could endanger the safety of the public surrounding the plant."[37] And one NRC official stated, not long ago, that "Several people with high explosives who really know how to use it can probably go through a nuclear facility like butter."[38]

According to testimony by Dr. Joseph M. Hendrie, chairman of the U.S. Nuclear Regulatory Commission:

> Our thinking has led NRC to conclude that the possibility of terrorist interest in a nuclear capability cannot be discounted. . . . Domestic nuclear power plants, as well as other major industrial installations, are also conceivable targets for terrorist action. To protect against the sabotage of a plant, licensees are required to use safeguards measures similar to the measures described above for the protection of special nuclear materials. The potential theft of nuclear plant fuel by terrorists is not a central concern because such fuel is not suitable for use by terrorists in a nuclear explosive. We are currently working with power plant licensees to implement strengthened security plans and procedures against sabotage which we required by rulemaking last year.[39]

The Nuclear Regulatory Commission has supported studies to determine the probable consequences of nuclear reactor

accidents and the kinds of safety systems needed to prevent
such accidents. While these studies do not deal with sabotage
as such, they do point out that (1) reactor safety systems
designed to prevent accidents also serve to prevent sabotage;
and (2) the worst consequences from nuclear reactor sabotage
would not exceed the worst cases from accidents. The *Reactor
Safety Study* (WASH-1400), known popularly as the Rasmussen Report of October 1975, indicates the dual-purpose safety
benefits of heavy shielding, thick-walled pipes and vessels,
features that cause shutdown of the chain reaction and con-
tinuance of core cooling, and restraints on piping and components to provide resistance to earthquakes. Although the
report does not calculate the actual risk from sabotage of nuclear
power plants, since the probability of such sabotage cannot be
estimated with any reliability, it does affirm the importance
of the issue. This affirmation is corroborated by the report of
the Risk Assessment Review Group, chartered by the Nuclear
Regulatory Commission in July 1977 to evaluate the Rasmussen Report.[40]

These views of nuclear reactor sabotage must be coupled with
the understanding that there have already been at least ninety-
four incidents involving threats of violence or acts of violence to
licensed nuclear facilities in this country since 1969. And there
have been at least ninety-one incidents during that time of
threats or acts of violence to unlicensed nuclear facilities. These
have not been idle threats. They have included pipe bombs
found near reactors, break-ins, and breaching of security perim-
eters. [41]

A number of security breaches are on record for the Three
Mile Island facility of the Metropolitan Edison Company in
Pennsylvania. On January 27, 1976, an intruder scaled the
security fence and entered the protected area of the installation.
Later, he drove off without being apprehended. Bomb threats
to this installation have been received on September 25, 1972;
March 23, 1973; and November 5, 1973.[42]

A significant number of acts of sabotage have taken place at nuclear facilities in other countries. Most of the installations involved are in Argentina, France, England, Scotland, Canada, and West Germany. Representative types of damage include cut wires, slashed gauges, dials, and electrical cables, smashed copper tubing, and serious fires.[43] Very recently, saboteurs bombed an industrial plant in France where two experimental nuclear reactors for Iraq were under construction. The three plastic explosive shells reportedly caused several million dollars in damage.

Terrorist Inclinations to Nuclear Violence

Observing the behavior of modern terrorists, one is reminded of the world pointed up by William Butler Yeats's poem, *The Second Coming,* a world in which "the worst are full of passionate intensity, while the best lack all conviction." Displaying an orientation to violence that has been shaped largely by the teachings of Sorel, Fanon, and Bakhunin, many of today's terrorist groups have abandoned the idea of distinguishing between combatants and noncombatants.[44] As a result of this inhuman calculus, the mad fury of terrorist activities has occasioned the killing and maiming of a great many innocent people.

The unwillingness to create boundaries in the threat and use of violence—an unwillingness that suggests a serious likelihood of nuclear terrorism should access to nuclear weapons or nuclear power plants be afforded insurgent groups—is the essence of terrorism. The mere threat or use of force for political ends does not signify the operation of terrorism.[45] It is always necessary that such force be threatened or applied *indiscriminately.*

Ironically, this meaning of terrorism was perhaps better understood by Aristotle than by most modern political scientists. Writing about the species of fear that arises from tragedy, Aristotle emphasized that such fear "demands a person who suffers undeservedly" and that it must be felt by "one of ourselves." This fear, or terror, has nothing to do with our concern for an impending misfortune to others, but from our perceived resemblance to the victim. We feel terror on *our own* behalf; we fear that we may ourselves become the objects of commiseration. Terror, in short, is fear referred back to ourselves.

Of course, Aristotle's *Poetics* does not deal with political terrorism, and the feelings of theatrical catharsis bear no direct resemblance to the sentiments of modern observers of terrorist violence. Yet, in the metaphorical sense, we are all involuntary playgoers at a continuous performance of the absurd drama of global political life. Thus riveted to the "stage," we require a far better awareness of what could happen, a far-reaching lucidity that can anticipate and prevent a frightful coup de theatre. To do this, we must understand, with Aristotle, that the purpose of the play is not to excite us with the misfortunes of fellow creatures, but to awaken within us fear for ourselves.

To a certain extent, the no-holds-barred orientation to violence of terrorists stems from pragmatic motives. Faced with a struggle that is typically cast as a zero-sum game, the terrorist suspends those norms of law that customarily mitigate the excesses of armed conflict, and embraces the imperative of a "war of annihilation." Since coexistence and compromise are judged impossible, all efforts are bent toward cataclysmic violence. In the case of Al Fatah, the apocalyptic "battle of vengeance" will galvanize the masses to "feel their active personality and restore their self-confidence."[46]

The no-holds-barred orientation to violence of many modern terrorist groups also stems from the romanticization of brutality that is a dominant motif of terrorist thinking. Even where it is doubtful that excessive and arbitrary force will be productive of their desired goals, terrorists are sometimes moved by Fanon's statement: "Violence is a purifying force. It frees the native from his inferiority complex and from despair and inaction. It makes him fearless and restores his self-respect."

This idea, that violence serves not only to injure the opposition but also to transform the revolutionary struggle, lies at the heart of the doctrine of Al Fatah. Any reading of Fatah pamphlets, e.g., "The Revolution and Violence, the Road to Victory,"

will reveal the influence of Frantz Fanon. Violence, the reader
is told, liberates not only through liquidation of the enemy, but
through its therapeutic and purifying effect *on the revolutionary*. Violence, states a Fatah memorandum to Arab journalists,
"is a healing medicine for all our people's diseases."[47]

Another basis of the no-holds-barred orientation to violence
that is present in modern terrorism lies in the position, articulated by many terrorist groups, that the overwhelming righteous-
ness of their objectives justifies any means whatsoever. Here,
of course, terrorists are engaged in the well-known argument,
"The ends justify the means." The contemporary roots of this
argument may be found in Mikhail Bakhunin's elucidation of
banditry in nineteenth-century Russia:

> The nature of Russian banditry is cruel and ruthless; yet no less
> cruel and ruthless is that governmental might which has brought this
> kind of bandit into being by its wanton acts. Governmental cruelty
> has engendered the cruelty of the people and made it into something
> necessary and natural. But between these two cruelties, there still
> remains a vast difference; the first strives for the complete annihila-
> tion of the people, the other endeavors to set them free.[48]

As long as terrorist groups assume such a stance on violent
excesses, they are susceptible to what Hannah Arendt has called
the "banality of evil" problem. This is the problem in which
individuals engage in evil without experiencing it as evil. In
certain instances, this problem has even occasioned terrorists
to displace responsibility for their own violent acts upon their
victims.

Witness, for example, the case of the shooting down of an
Air Rhodesia Viscount turboprop plane with fifty-nine people
on board in February 1979. Acknowledging that the plane had
been fired upon by his followers, Joshua Nkomo, the Zambia-
based coleader of the Patriotic Front guerrillas, stopped short of
accepting responsibility. This would have to be accepted, he
argued, by the Rhodesian defense chief, Lt. General Peter Walls,
who the guerrillas had reason to believe was traveling on the

plane. (In fact, Walls had left Kariba Airport for Salisbury on a second aircraft, one that left fifteen minutes after the unfortunate flight, RH-827.) Insisted Nkomo, only Walls was "responsible for the deaths of all these other people because he is the biggest military target."[49]

Many of today's terrorists are able to avoid individual responsibility for their acts by displacing this responsibility upon the terrorist group itself. By transforming persons into members of the group, i.e., into servants of a "higher cause," feelings of individual responsibility have been submerged by the "psychology of the cell." The effects of this "psychology" increase the likelihood of nuclear terrorism.

Of course, the displacement of individual responsibility for barbaric acts from individual to group was "perfected" by Hitler's SS. There, under the direction of Heinrich Himmler's "official" terrorism, such displacement reached its twentieth-century apotheosis. Acting as the principal enforcer of the "Final Solution," Himmler, addressing an assemblage of *Einsatzkommandos* ("extermination commandos") in the late summer of 1941, pointed out that the men taking part in the liquidation bore no personal responsibility for their acts. Rather, the responsibility was entirely his and the führer's. According to the testimony at Nuremberg of Otto Ohlendorf, head of Bureau III of the Reich Main Security Office and commander of an *Einsatzgruppe* in the east:

> Himmler was in Nikolaev in the late summer of 1941. He summoned the leaders and men of the *Einsatzkommandos* and repeated to them the order for liquidation and stressed that leaders and men who were concerned in these measures did not carry any personal responsibility for carrying them out. He alone, and the Führer, bore this responsibility.[50]

Terrorist Insensitivity to Orthodox Deterrence

In Act 2 of his play *Henry IV*, Luigi Pirandello reminds us that not all of the players in life's game always abide by the rules, and that calculations that rest upon the foundations of logic crumble before madness: "Do you know what it means to find yourselves face to face with a madman—with one who shakes the foundations of all you have built up in yourselves, your logic, the logic of all your constructions? Madmen, lucky folk, construct without logic, or rather with a logic that flies like a feather."

Understood in terms of the problem of nuclear terrorism, Pirandello's wisdom suggests the irrelevance of conventional deterrence "logic" as an effective preventive strategy. Although it would be unreasonable to suggest that all terrorists are mad and irrational, it would not be unreasonable to suggest that terrorist groups typically operate under a special meaning of rationality. Indeed, terrorist operatives are sometimes even willing to "die for the cause." This renders them insensitive to the kinds of retaliatory threats that are the traditional mainstay of order between states.

What are the implications of this particular behavioral characteristic of terrorist actors for the threat of nuclear terrorism? Clearly, the most important implication is that terrorists calculating the prospective costs and benefits of nuclear insurgency might ignore the fear of retaliatory destruction. This means that traditional threats of deterrence might have little or no bearing on the terrorist decision concerning the use of nuclear force.

A willingness to "die for the cause" also creates martyrs, which can be helpful to the terrorist purpose. This idea has been best understood by the terrorist theoretician, Abraham Guillen:

> In a revolutionary war a guerrilla action that needs explaining to the people is politically useless: it should be meaningful and convincing by itself. To kill an ordinary soldier in reprisal for the assassination of a guerrilla is to descend to the same political level as a reactionary army. Far better to create a martyr and thereby attract mass sympathy than to lose or neutralize popular support by senseless killings without an evident political goal.[51]

Although far less instrumental in his understanding of martyrdom in the context of insurgency, Herbert Marcuse also recognizes the martyr's contribution:

> Martyrs have rarely helped a political cause, and "revolutionary suicide" remains suicide. And yet, it would be self-righteous indifference to say that the revolutionary ought to live rather than die for the revolution—an insult to the Communards of all times. When the establishment proclaims its professional killers as heroes, and its rebelling victims as criminals, it is hard to save the idea of heroism for the other side. The desperate act, doomed to failure, may for a brief moment tear the veil of justice and expose the faces of brutal suppression; it may arouse the conscience of the neutrals; it may reveal hidden cruelties and lies. Only he who commits the desperate act can judge whether the price he is bound to pay is too high.[52]

Perhaps the most frightening implication of self-sacrificing behavior on the part of terrorists is the idea that similar behavior might be needed for successful counterterrorism. Writing from a fundamentally different ideological point of view than Guillen and Marcuse, but in much the same analytic vein, Gerald Priestland offers the following novel observation:

> What the free world has to realise is that, if it wants to remain free, it will, besides maintaining police vigilance, have to accept civilian casualties. Sooner or later someone will have to give the order to assault a hijacked plane, hostages or no hostages—refuse to release convicted terrorists, whatever the blackmail—turn down demands for aviation fuel, whether or not the plane is blown up in retaliation. If innocent hostages are killed—well, there can never be any adequate solace in any kind of bereavement. But the free world should honor those victims as martyrs in the cause of freedom, and see that their dependants are taken care of even more generously than those of soldiers who fall in battle. Those are hard words to write; but this is the knot of the problem: if men are ready to die for what is wrong, how can the right triumph unless its supporters are ready to die too?[53]

Even where terrorists do not display self-sacrificing characteristics, their unique stance on the balance of risks that can be taken renders them insensitive to orthodox threats of deterrence.

Since their willingness to take risks is usually far greater than that of states, the prevention of nuclear terrorism will have to take this into account. In this connection, it is essential that deterrent measures be correlated with the particular terrorist stance on the balance of risks that can be taken. Instead of the usual threats of physically punishing retaliation, deterrence of nuclear terrorism must be based upon threats to obstruct circumstances that terrorists value even more than personal safety.

These circumstances center upon sectors of public support for terrorist goals and strategies. In this connection, one is reminded of the "hunger artist" in Franz Kafka's novella of the same name. For the hunger artist, a professional faster, sustained starvation was hardly a form of punishment. After all, he had—as is made clear in the story—no real appetite for food. However, once his regular coterie of observers and admirers began to drift away from their daily vigil as an enthusiastic audience, he quickly shriveled and died. His true punishment, and the actual cause of his death, lay not in starvation, but in the withdrawal of people from whose admiring looks and exaltations the hunger artist drew his only meaningful nourishment.

In the manner of Kafka's strange character, certain of today's terrorist groups typically fear the withdrawal of popular interest and support more acutely than threats to their physical lives. It follows that since their "appetite" for life may actually be subordinate to the need for popular adulation, the key to successful deterrence of nuclear terrorism lies less in the threat of physical harm than in the removal of an admiring public. To reduce the probability of terrorist nuclear violence, threats should be considered that recognize the wisdom of Kafka's story.

Interterrorist Cooperation

There exists a new phenomenon in world politics—systematic cooperation and collaboration between terrorist groups. Terrorists have always formed alignments with sympathetic states, but now they are also beginning to cement patterns of alliance with each other. In recent years, a significant number of joint operations have taken place. Most of these cooperative cadres of multinational operational teams have involved the Popular Front for the Liberation of Palestine (PFLP). Consider the following events:

May 1972. Japanese Red Army (JRA)/PFLP/German collaboration in attacking Lod Airport, Israel.

July 1973. PFLP/JRA/Latin American cooperation in hijacking a Japan Air Lines 747 aircraft in Europe.

January 1974. PFLP/JRA operation against Shell Oil facilities in Singapore.

September 1974. JRA/PFLP/Baader-Meinhof collaboration in assault on the French Embassy, The Hague.

January 1975. PFLP/German/Carlos cooperation in attempted attack against El Al aircraft, Orly Airport, Paris.

December 1975. Carlos/German/Palestinian collaboration in the Vienna assault on the ministerial conference of the Oil Producing and Exporting Countries (OPEC).

June 1976. PFLP/Latin American/German effort culminating at Entebbe.[54]

What are the implications of such cooperation for nuclear destruction by terrorists?

First, interterrorist cooperation vastly increases terrorist opportunities for acquiring nuclear weapons. This is especially true when acquisition takes the form of self-development and design from "raw" fissionable materials, since cooperation expands opportunities for both capital and expertise.

Second, cooperation among terrorist groups is apt to encourage the spread of "private" nuclear weapons around the world, creating a network whereby such weapons can be exchanged and transported across national boundaries.

Third, cooperation between terrorists is likely to spread the "benefits" of advanced training in the use of nuclear weapons and the techniques of nuclear reactor sabotage.

Fourth, terrorist cooperation is likely to provide such reciprocal privileges as forged documents and safe-havens, which are needed for pre- and post-attack operations.

Fifth, since virtually all of the cooperative training of terrorists is conducted under Palestinian direction in Palestinian camps, such training is likely to enlarge the number of targets attractive to the Palestinians. To a certain extent, and as we have already noted, this enlargement has already taken place as Japanese Red Army, Latin American, and German groups have "repaid" George Habash's PFLP with attacks on Israeli personnel and facilities.[55]

Tolerance and Support of Terrorism

Ironically, while terrorists are engaged in "total war" encounters with much of humanity, the prevailing attitude in many countries is one of tolerance or open support. Consider just two prominent examples. First, in the wake of the July 4, 1976, Israeli commando raid at Entebbe, which freed 105 hostages taken by pro-Palestinian skyjackers, African members of the Security Council proposed a resolution to condemn the raid as a "flagrant violation" of Uganda's sovereignty. In view of long-standing international law, such a proposal was unjustified since all states have a responsibility to protect nationals of other countries and a corresponding obligation to protect their own nationals in extremis abroad. Second, in the aftermath of Munich, a number of Arab governments heaped lavish praise upon Black September for its attack on the Israeli athletes in the Olympic Village.

In international relations, the tolerance and support of terrorism by certain states stems from the belief that terrorist groups often work in their own national interests. Issues of morality are overshadowed by the presumption that terrorists, however inadvertently, are useful surrogates in the ongoing struggle for international power and influence.[56] The predictable end of such narrow-minded notions of this struggle has been presaged by earlier periods of human history in which global society has lost its center of values; by periods of frightful barbarism; and by periods still anticipated in Nietzsche's parable on the "death of God."

In Nietzsche's parable, a madman runs into a village square shouting, "Where is God?". Answering his own question, the madman proceeds to inform the laughing villagers: "God is dead! God remains dead! . . . and we have killed him! . . . I come too early. . . . This tremendous event is still on its way." The madman's "tremendous event" is nothing less than poet William Butler Yeats's description of *The Second Coming*:

> Things fall apart; the centre cannot hold;
> Mere anarchy is loosed upon the world,
> The blood-dimmed tide is loosed, and everywhere
> The ceremony of innocence is drowned.

In our own century, a period of human history whose dominant motif has been defined by Auschwitz, Hiroshima, and My Lai, this "tremendous event" is already well under way. With the development of alignments between states and terrorist groups in a nuclear age, we are now only moments away from its apocalyptic conclusion.

At the moment, a number of countries—e.g., Libya, Saudi Arabia, Somalia, Kuwait, Iraq, Syria, South Yemen, Algeria, Vietnam, and the Soviet Bloc[57]—are committed sponsors of such alignments. Recently, these countries were joined by Iran, which, under the new Islamic government of the Ayatollah Khomeini, has pledged its support to the Palestinian insurgency against Israel, and turned over the Israeli embassy to Yasser Arafat's PLO. As long as this situation prevails, many terrorist groups will continue to interpret aid from sponsor states as an incentive to violence.

The idea of terrorism as surrogate political warfare is hardly a recent development. Even before the 1960s, when state-supported terrorism became commonplace in the Middle East and North Africa, Italian fascists supported the Croatian *Ustasha* in the assassination of King Alexander in 1934.[58] Today, the surrogate phenomenon has been widely termed "a new type of war," and has received considerable attention in the scholarly literature.

In a Rand Corporation paper published by Brian Jenkins in June 1974, the author points out that "Although the actual amount of violence caused by international terrorism is small compared with war, it has had a destabilizing effect on international order and could become a surrogate for conventional warfare against a nation."[59] According to Jenkins:

> Terrorists, whatever their origin or cause, have demonstrated the possibilities of . . . "surrogate warfare." Terrorism, though now rejected as a legitimate mode of warfare by most conventional military establishments, could become an accepted form of warfare in the future. Terrorists could be employed to provoke international incidents, create alarm in an adversary's country, compel it to divert valuable resources to protect itself, destroy its morale, and carry out specific acts of sabotage. Governments could employ existing terrorist groups to attack their opponents, or they could create their own terrorists. Terrorism requires only a small investment, certainly far less than what it costs to wage conventional war. It can be debilitating to the enemy.[60]

A recent CIA study, however, takes exception to the idea that surrogate warfare will become increasingly likely. According to the study:

> barring total collapse of world order and consequent international anarchy (something that no state actor has reason to promote), international terrorism is highly unlikely to gain acceptance as an admissable form of behavior in the forseeable future. All told, in fact, it seems likely that the employment of terrorist groups in a surrogate warfare role will continue to be more the exception than the rule for some time to come.[61]

This conclusion is regrettably unconvincing, however, since it flows from the erroneous premises that (1) states identify their own interests with the continued operation of the international legal order, and (2) states identify their support of terrorism with the total collapse of that order.

A more compelling argument is offered by Russell E. Bigney and others, in their "Exploration of the Nature of Future Warfare":

> The costs and destructiveness of modern warfare, including insurgent wars, are becoming prohibitive and may exceed net gains. As a result, many nations are looking for alternative means to achieve political and economic dominance over adversary nations. The relative low cost of sponsored terrorism and the disproportionate influence that a small well-trained terrorist group can exert becomes an attractive alternative to war.[62]

Support of international terrorism is also increased to the extent that terrorists influence the foreign policies of "host" states. For example, the host states, sometimes in combination with allied countries, may act as advocates of the terrorist groups before the "tribunal" of the state system itself. Such advocacy further legitimizes terrorists as actors in world politics, extending their arena of acceptance and influence.

In 1974, the PLO was internationally recognized as the sole legitimate representative of the Palestinian people. The PLO has also been admitted into the UN's ECWA (Economic Commission of Western Asia) and has been granted observer status with such other UN-affiliated agencies as WHO (World Health Organization), ILO (International Labor Organization), UPU (Universal Postal Union), ITU (International Telecommunication Union), and UNESCO (United Nations Educational, Scientific, and Cultural Organization). Moreover, it has been able to open offices in over fifty nations. Such action, like the Khomeini transfer to the PLO of the Israeli Embassy in Tehran, has the effect of making a terrorist organization a "juristic person," and heightens terrorist incentives to nuclear violence.

Proposals to sever the bonds between states and terrorist groups are often based on the idea that all states have a common interest in combatting terrorism. These proposals rest on the erroneous premise that all states value the secure operation of the international diplomatic system more than any objective that might be obtained via terrorist surrogates. Such a premise has its roots in—and is affirmed by—a basic principle of international law: that is, the legal systems embodied in the constitutions of particular states are part of the international legal order, and are therefore an interest that all states must defend against attack.

In support of this principle, most texts and treatises on international law express the opinion that a state is forbidden to allow its territory to be used as a base for aggressive operations against another state with which it is not at war. Building upon the writings of such luminaries as Liszt, Oppenheim, Calvo, Rivier, Pradier-Fodéré, Fauchille, De Louter, Alvarez, and Redslob, Hersch Lauterpacht formulates the following rule concerning the scope of state responsibility for preventing and repressing revolutionary acts of private persons against foreign states:

> International law imposes upon the State the duty of restraining persons within its territory from engaging in such revolutionary activities against friendly States as amount to organized acts of force in the form of hostile expeditions against the territory of those States. It also obliges the State to repress and discourage activities in which attempts against the life of political opponents are regarded as a proper means of revolutionary action.[63]

Lauterpacht's rule reaffirms the *Resolution on the Rights and Duties of Foreign Powers as regards the Established and Recognized Governments in case of Insurrection* adopted by the Institute of International Law in 1900. (Section 3 of Article 2 prohibits states to allow a hostile military expedition against an established and recognized government to be organized within its territory.) However, even in obligating states to actively oppose insurgency directed against other states, his rule falls short of the prescription offered by the eighteenth century Swiss scholar, Emerich de Vattel. According to Book 2 of Vattel's *The Law of Nations,* states that support such insurgency become the lawful prey of other states:

> If there should be found a restless and unprincipled nation, ever ready to do harm to others, to thwart their purposes, and to stir up civil strife among their citizens, there is no doubt that all others would have the right to unite together to subdue such a nation, to discipline it, and even to disable it from doing further harm.

3
Nuclear Terrorism:
Forms and Effects

Nietzsche, in the long critique of faith in his *AntiChrist,* writes: " 'Faith' means not *wanting* to know what is true." Understood in terms of humankind's continuing obliviousness to its own self-destruct tendencies, Nietzsche's point suggests not only cowardice, but also a long-prophesied *Götterdämmerung.* Unless we begin to experience some widespread shocks of recognition about our current nuclear collision course, there is little hope that humankind can escape its last paroxysm.

Spasmodic instances of awareness are not enough. If we are to prevent nuclear catastrophe in world politics, we must begin immediately to hone our anticipatory imagination of what it could entail. The wreckage of moral, spiritual, and physical well-being that would descend in the wake of nuclear terrorism (wreckage that, we shall see, could include nuclear war) must be made more visible if it is to be avoided.

The ground is slowly dissolving under our feet, but we are either unaware of the situation or pretend not to notice. Our pretenses, everyone's pretenses, that irretrievable nuclear disaster cannot happen represent a fatal flight from reality. Our only hope for survival lies in facing the awesome possibilities squarely, and in transforming our primal terrors into constructive strategies of prevention.

Humankind's tendency to flee from a seemingly intolerable reality is communicated brilliantly in Doris Lessing's novel, *The Memoirs of a Survivor.* Amidst a dark vision of the not-so-distant future, when humanity gropes for security in a rapidly disintegrating world, the narrator captures our species' peculiar penchant for collective self-delusion:

> For instance, on the newscasts and in the papers they would pursue for days the story of a single kidnapped child, taken from its pram perhaps by some poor unhappy woman. The police would be combing the suburbs and the countryside in hundreds, looking for the child, and for the woman, to punish her. But the next news flash would be about the mass deaths of hundreds, thousands, or even millions of people. We still believed, wanted to believe, that the first—the concern about the single child, the need to punish the individual criminal, even if it took days and weeks and hundreds of our hard-worked police force to do it—was what really represented us; the second, about the catastrophe, was, as such items of news had always been for people not actually in the threatened area, an unfortunate and minor—or at least not crucial—accident, which interrupted the even flow, the development, of civilization.

There are fissures in the columns of false hopes that sustain our unsteady civilization. These fissures must be enlarged, and the entire edifice of empty expectations destroyed, if a more enduring structure of global society is to be erected. Humankind must learn to spark and nurture deep intimations of a post-catastrophe future as an essential step toward averting such a future. To accomplish this, we must look unflinchingly at the full, unvarnished consequences of nuclear terrorism.

This chapter portrays a landscape of dread. The vision of this landscape will appear cadaverous. But it must not make us dispirited! Quite the contrary. It must supply us with the motive and the momentum to reorder our hierarchy of concerns.

The kind of playacting described in Lessing's novel can no longer be tolerated in a world teetering at the abyss. The smell of death saturates the air. If it is ignored, we will succumb, not to its repellent olfactory stimuli, but to the blasted orgy of collapse that it forewarns. If it is heeded, as a final presentiment of our species' convulsive rendezvous with extinction, its bitter scent can transform latent potentialities into prodigious efforts at renewal.

In the unsentimental theater of modern world politics, the time is at hand for a new kind of dramaturgy, a "new naturalism" that touches profoundly the deepest rhythms of human imagination. At the same time, we must resurrect the traditional function of theater to evoke pity and terror. The world is pregnant with apocalyptic possibilities. These possibilities must be acknowledged forthrightly, with ruthless frankness, and without sentimentality or shamefaced absentmindedness.

Nuclear Explosives

The low-technology nuclear explosives that might be manufactured by terrorists could range anywhere from a few hundred tons to several kilotons in yield. The destructive potential of such explosives would depend upon such variables as type of construction, population density, prevailing wind direction, weather patterns, and the characteristic features of the target area. Such potential would be manifested in terms of three primary effects: *blast* (measured in pounds per square inch of overpressure); *heat* (measured in calories/cm^2); and *radiation* (measured in Radiation Effective Man—REM—a combined measure that includes the Radiation Absorbed Dose—RAD—and the Radiation Biological Effectiveness—RBE—or the varying biological effectiveness of different types of radiation).

Relatively crude nuclear explosives with yields equivalent to about 1,000 tons of high explosive would be far easier to fabricate than explosives with yields equivalent to about 10 kilotons of high explosive.[1] Nonetheless, explosives with a yield of only 1/10 of a kiloton would pose significant destructive effects. A nuclear explosive in this "limited range" could annihilate the Capitol during the State of the Union Address or knock down the World Trade Center towers in New York City. An even smaller yield of 10 tons of TNT could kill everyone attending the Super Bowl.[2]

In assessing the destructiveness of nuclear explosions, it is important to remember that such explosions are typically more damaging than chemical explosions of equivalent yields. This is the case because nuclear explosions produce energy in the form of penetrating radiations (gamma rays and neutrons) as well as in blast wave and heat. Moreover, a nuclear explosion on the ground—the kind of nuclear explosion most likely to be used by terrorists—produces *more* local fallout than a comparable explosion in the air.[3]

Radiological Weapons

Radiological weapons are not as widely understood as nuclear explosives, but they are equally ominous in their effects. Placed in the hands of terrorists, such weapons could pose a lethal hazard for human beings anywhere in the world. Even a world already dominated by every variety of numbing could not fail to recoil in horror from such a prospect.

Radiological weapons are devices designed to disperse radioactive materials that have been produced a substantial time before their dispersal. The targets against which terrorists might choose to use radiological weapons include concentrations of people inside buildings, concentrations of people on urban streets or at sports events, urban areas with a high population density as a whole, and agricultural areas.[4] The form such weapons might take include plutonium dispersal devices (only 3½ ounces of plutonium could prove lethal to everyone within a large office building or factory) or devices designed to disperse other radioactive materials. In principle, the dispersal of spent nuclear reactor fuel and the fission products separated from reactor fuels would create grave hazards in a populated area, but the handling of such materials would be very dangerous to terrorists themselves. It is more likely, therefore, that would-be users of radiological weapons would favor plutonium over radioactive fission products.[5]

The threat of nuclear terrorism involving radiological weapons is potentially more serious than the threat involving nuclear explosives. This is a fact, because it would be easier for terrorists to achieve nuclear capability with radiological weapons. Such weapons, therefore, could also be the subject of a more plausible hoax than nuclear explosives.

Nuclear Reactor Sabotage

In the aftermath of the Three Mile Island near-catastrophe, even the average layperson is familiar with the meaning of "reactor-core meltdown." Such an event, in which a reactor deprived of its temperature-controlling coolant melts in its own heat and produces lethal clouds of radioactive gases, could be the objective of future terrorism. As we have already noted, incidents involving violence or threats of violence at nuclear facilities at home and abroad are already a matter of record.

In comparison to a low-yield nuclear explosion, a reactor-core meltdown and breach of containment would release a small amount of radiation.[6] However, the consequences of such an event would still involve leakage of an immense amount of gaseous radioactive material that could expose neighboring populations to immediate death, cancer, or genetic defects. To better understand the nature of the threat, one must first try to understand the fundamentals of nuclear reactors.

Essentially, these reactors may be characterized as giant teakettles that turn water into steam. The steam is piped to large turbines that turn generators. When a typical "teakettle" is operating at full power, the radioactivity in its fuel core can reach 17 billion curies, enough—in principle—to kill everyone on the planet. Within the uranium fuel rods in the core, the fission reaction can unleash energy to drive the temperature above 4,000 degrees Farenheit—a temperature hot enough to melt through all protective barriers.[7]

In assessing the dangers of nuclear power reactors, the Rasmussen Report expects an extremely serious accident (which would closely resemble sabotage in its effects) to produce 3,300 prompt fatalities, 45,000 instances of early illness, 240,000 thyroid nodules over a thirty-year period, and 30,000 genetic defects over one hundred and fifty years. Additionally, the economic loss due to contamination over an area of 3,200 square miles is estimated at $14 billion.[8]

On July 1, 1977, the U.S. Nuclear Regulatory Commission organized the Risk Assessment Review Group. The group's purpose was to "clarify the achievements and limitations of the Rasmussen Report, WASH-1400, to study the state of such risk assessment methodology, and to recommend whether and how such methodology can be used in the licensing and regulation of reactors."[9] The group concluded that WASH-1400 had been conservative in certain respects, particularly as regards the overall probability of core melt.

While finding WASH-1400 to be "a conscientious and honest effort" to assess nuclear reactor safety,[10] the Risk Assessment Review Group identified nagging doubts about that effort's probability calculations. Among these doubts, the following is highlighted in the group's summary:

> inability to quantify human adaptability during the course of an accident, and a pervasive regulatory influence in the choice of uncertain parameters, while among the latter are nagging issues about completeness, and an inadequate treatment of common cause failure. We are unable to define whether the overall probability of a core melt given in WASH-1400 is high or low, but we are certain that the error bands are understated. We cannot say by how much. Reasons for this include an inadequate data base, a poor statistical treatment, an inconsistent propagation of uncertainties throughout the calculation, etc.[11]

In the group's statement of findings, WASH-1400 is characterized, despite its stated shortcomings, as "the most complete single picture of accident probabilities associated with nuclear reactors." At the same time, the following points were also made.

• The dispersion model for radioactive material developed in WASH-1400 for reactor sites as a class cannot be applied to individual sites without significant refinement and sensitivity tests.

• The biological effects models should be updated and improved in the light of new information.

• After having studied the peer comments about some important classes of initiating events, we are unconvinced of the correctness of the WASH-1400 conclusion that they contribute negligibly to the overall risk. Examples include fires, earthquakes, and human accident initiation.

• The statistical analysis in WASH-1400 leaves much to be desired. It suffers from a spectrum of problems, ranging from lack of data on which to base input distributions to the invention and use of wrong statistical methods. Even when the analysis is done correctly, it is often presented in so murky a way as to be very hard to decipher.

• For a report of this magnitude, confidence in the correctness of the results can only come from a systematic and deep peer review process. The peer review process of WASH-1400 was defective in many ways and the review was inadequate.

• Lack of scrutability is a major failing of the report, impairing both its usefulness and the quality of possible peer review.

• The Executive Summary to WASH-1400, which is by far the most widely read part of the report among the public and policy makers, does not adequately indicate the full extent of the consequences of reactor accidents; and does not sufficiently emphasize the uncertainties involved in the calculation of their probability. It has therefore lent itself to misuse in the discussion of reactor risk.

• WASH-1400 was directed to make a "realistic" estimate of risk. In the regulatory process, the usual conservatisms must be incorporated. There have been instances in which WASH-1400 has been misused as a vehicle to judge the acceptability of reactor risks. In other cases, it may have been used prematurely as an estimate of the absolute risk of reactor accidents without full realization of the wide band of uncertainties involved. Such use should be discouraged.[12]

Whatever form nuclear terrorism might take—nuclear explosives, radiological weapons, or nuclear reactor sabotage—its effects would be social and political as well as biological and physical. In the aftermath of a nuclear terrorist event, both governments and insurgents would be confronted with mounting pressures to escalate to higher-order uses of force. With terrorists more inclined to think of nuclear weapons as manifestly "thinkable," both governments and terrorists would find themselves giving serious consideration to striking first.

Like Caligula, who kills because "there's only one way of getting even with the gods . . . to be as cruel as they," a number of terrorist groups would turn to nuclear weaponry as a promising new instrument of vengeance. Faced with such madness, governments would find it necessary to choreograph their own macabre dances of death, meeting savagery with savagery in a quest for security that might reveal only impotence. In the wake of such widespread dislocation, madness would be celebrated by all sides as the liberating core of survival, and sanity would dissolve into insignificance.

It is not a pretty picture. The record of human history reveals not only the most extreme manifestations of deliberate evil, but also the most bizarre and inexplicable attraction to that evil. Living, as we must, with both the memory and the expectation of holocaust, the "pornography of death" that lies latent in the prospect of nuclear terrorism carries not only the dark vision of cosmic disorder, but also the deformation of the human spirit through successive imitations of excessive violence.

Nuclear Terrorism and Nuclear War

Nuclear terrorism could even spark full-scale nuclear war between states. Such war could involve the entire spectrum of nuclear conflict possibilities, ranging from a nuclear attack upon a nonnuclear state to systemwide nuclear war. How might such far-reaching consequences of nuclear terrorism come about? Perhaps the most likely way would involve a terrorist nuclear assault against a state by terrorists "hosted" in another state. For example, consider the following scenario:

Early in the 1980s, Israel and her Arab state neighbors finally stand ready to conclude a comprehensive, multilateral peace settlement. With a bilateral treaty between Israel and Egypt already several years old, only the interests of the Palestinians—as defined by the PLO—seem to have been left out. On the eve of the proposed signing of the peace agreement, half a dozen crude nuclear explosives in the one-kiloton range detonate in as many Israeli cities. Public grief in Israel over the many thousand dead and maimed is matched only by the outcry for revenge. In response to the public mood, the government of Israel initiates selected strikes against terrorist strongholds in Lebanon, whereupon the Lebanese government and its allies retaliate against Israel. Before long, the entire region is ablaze, conflict has escalated to nuclear forms, and all countries in the area have suffered unprecedented destruction.

Of course, such a scenario is fraught with the makings of even wider destruction. How would the United States react to the situation in the Middle East? What would be the Soviet response? It is certainly conceivable that a chain reaction of interstate nuclear conflict could ensue, one that would ultimately involve the superpowers or even every nuclear weapon state on the planet.

What, exactly, would this mean? Whether the terms of assessment be statistical or human, the consequences of nuclear war require an entirely new paradigm of death. Only such a paradigm would allow us a proper framework for absorbing the vision of near-total obliteration and the outer limits of human destructiveness. Any nuclear war would have effectively permanent and irreversible consequences. Whatever the actual extent of injuries and fatalities, it would entomb the spirit of the entire species in a planetary casket strewn with shorn bodies and imbecile imaginations.

This would be as true for a "limited" nuclear war as for an "unlimited" one. Contrary to continuing Pentagon commitments to the idea of selected "counterforce" strikes that would reduce the chances for escalation and produce fewer civilian casualties, the strategy of limited nuclear war is inherently unreasonable. There is, in fact, no clear picture of what states might hope to gain from counterforce attacks. This understanding is reflected by Soviet military strategy, which is founded on the idea that any nuclear conflict would necessarily be unlimited.

Nuclear War Between the Superpowers

The consequences of a strategic exchange between the United States and the Soviet Union have been the object of widespread attention. One account of these consequences is offered by Andrei D. Sakharov, the brilliant physicist who played a leading role in the development of Russia's thermonuclear capacity:

> A complete destruction of cities, industry, transport, and systems of education, a poisoning of fields, water, and air by radioactivity, a physical destruction of the larger part of mankind, poverty, barbarism, a return to savagery, and a genetic degeneracy of the survivors under the impact of radiation, a destruction of the material and information basis of civilization—this is a measure of the peril that threatens the world as a result of the estrangement of the world's two superpowers.[13]

Presently, U.S. strategic arsenals contain approximately 9,000 strategic weapons and 4,000 megaton equivalents. Soviet strategic forces number approximately 3,000 weapons and about 5,000 megaton equivalents.[14] An exchange involving any substantial fraction of these forces could promptly destroy more than half of the urban populations in both countries. The subsequent fallout could be expected to kill upwards of 50 percent of the surviving rural inhabitants as well as create worldwide contamination of the atmosphere.[15]

To better understand the effects of fallout, it is useful to recognize that radiation effects have three basic forms: (1) radiation directly from the explosion; (2) immediate radioactive fallout (first twenty-four hours); and (3) long-term fallout (months and years). In areas where radioactive fallout is of particularly high intensity, individuals will be exposed to high doses of radiation regardless of shelter protection. Those who do not become prompt or short-term fatalities and have suffered radiation exposures above 100 REMs will undergo hemotological (blood system) alterations that diminish immunological capabilities. The resultant vulnerability to infection will seriously impair prospects for long-term recovery.[16]

The effects of a nuclear war between the superpowers, however, cannot be understood solely in terms of projected casualties. Rather, these effects must also include *quantitative* effects (i.e., availability of productive capacity, fuel, labor, food, and other resources); *qualitative* effects (i.e., political, social, and psychological damage); and *interactive* effects (i.e., the impact on the relationships between the social and economic factors of production).[17] When these corollary effects are taken into account, it is easy to see that policy makers and public alike have typically understated the aggregate impact of nuclear war.

This point is supported by a 1975 study of the National Research Council, National Academy of Sciences, entitled *Long-Term Worldwide Effects of Multiple Nuclear Weapons Detonations.* Going beyond the usual litany of crude physical measures of destruction (e.g., number of human fatalities, number of cities destroyed), the report portrays the *long-term, worldwide* effects following a hypothetical exchange of 10,000 megatons of explosive power in the northern hemisphere. These effects are cast in terms of atmosphere and climate, natural terrestrial ecosystems, agriculture and animal husbandry, the aquatic environment, and both somatic and genetic changes in human populations.[18]

While the report recognizes that the biosphere and the species Homo sapiens would survive the hypothesized nuclear war, it recognizes that the very idea of survival in such a context is problematic. Building upon this recognition, a more recent study prepared for the Joint Committee on Defense Production of the Congress—*Economic and Social Consequences of Nuclear Attacks on the United States*—identifies four discrete levels of postattack survival. This new taxonomy permits a more subtle look at the interactive effects of nuclear war and allows more precise judgments about the acceptability or unacceptability of nuclear attack damage. According to the study, there are four levels of survival, in decreasing order of damage.

1. *Biological Survival of Individuals.* Individuals or groups of individuals survive but not necessarily within the organized political, social, and economic structure of a modern society.

2. *Regional Survival of Political Structures.* Some subnational political units survive as viable entities, but without a functioning central government.

3. *Survival of a Central Government.* Some form of viable, central control over all preattack national territory survives, but the effectiveness of this control may vary over an extremely wide range, depending on the specific nature and pattern of the attack(s).

4. *Survival Intact of Basic Societal Structure.* Damage to the nation is characterized as relatively limited socially, politically and economically; nevertheless, the attack is militarily destructive. This is the concept of survival envisioned in the notion of limited or controlled nuclear war. However, it should be noted that the idea that effective strategic military attacks can be benign in their impacts on society is in dispute. It is used here as a criterion without any implicit acceptance that it can be achieved.[19]

There are, however, levels of strategic exchange at which even the first listed category of survival might not be relevant. At such levels, the species itself—let alone organized political, social, and economic structures—would disappear. The plausibility of such levels is underscored by the fact that the magnitude of exchange postulated in the NAS report is really quite low. Were the superpowers to exchange between 50,000 and 100,000 megatons of nuclear explosives, rather than the 10,000 megatons assumed by the report, worldwide climatological changes would imperil the physical existence of Homo sapiens.

Worldwide Nuclear War

If nuclear terrorism should lead to worldwide nuclear war,

the results would represent humankind's last and most complete calamity, defying not only our imaginations of disaster, but our customary measurements as well. As the culmination of what Camus once described as "years of absolutely insane history," worldwide nuclear war would represent the final eradication of the very boundaries of annihilation.

In technical terms, the consequences of systemwide nuclear war would include atmospheric effects; effects on natural terrestrial ecosystems; effects on managed terrestrial ecosystems; and effects on the aquatic environment.

Atmospheric effects would be highlighted by greatly reduced ozone concentrations producing increased ultraviolet radiation and a drop in average temperature. Even the possibility of irreversible climatic shifts cannot be ruled out.[20]

Natural Terrestrial Ecosystems would be affected by systemwide nuclear war through three principal stress factors: ionizing radiation; uv-B radiation; and climatic change. The cumulative effect of these three factors would render the entire planet a "hot spot" where even vast forests would show physiological and genetic damage.[21]

Managed Terrestrial Ecosystems would be affected by systemwide nuclear war by radionuclide contamination of foods, chromosome breakage and gene mutations in crops, and yield-reducing sterility in seed crops. The cumulative effect of these changes would be the disappearance of the technology base for agriculture. Even if there were any significant number of human survivors, a return to normal world food production would be unimaginable.[22]

Aquatic effects of a systemwide nuclear war would stem from ionizing radiation from radionuclides in marine waters and freshwaters; solar uv radiation; and changes in water temperatures associated with climate. Irreversible injuries to sensitive aquatic species could be anticipated during the years of large transient increase in uv-B isolation. And the range of geographic distribution of sensitive populations of aquatic organisms could be reduced.[23]

Other Forms of Nuclear War

Nuclear war between the superpowers and worldwide nuclear war are only two forms of strategic conflict that might be sparked by nuclear terrorism. Other forms include a nuclear attack upon a nonnuclear state; a two-country strategic exchange involving secondary nuclear powers; nuclear exchanges between several secondary nuclear powers; nuclear exchanges between secondary nuclear powers and one of the superpowers; nuclear exchanges between secondary nuclear powers and both of the superpowers; and nuclear exchanges between secondary nuclear powers plus one of the superpowers on the one side and other secondary nuclear powers on the opposing side. Although there is apt to be a significant difference in consequences between these forms of nuclear war, some important regularities do emerge.

For example, whatever the kinds of weapons used, their yields, their altitudes of detonation, and the prevailing weather patterns, wide swaths of destruction would be produced by thermal radiation, nuclear radiation, and blast. Individuals would suffer flash and flame burns. Retinal burns could occur in the eyes of persons at distances of several hundred miles from the explosion. People would be crushed by collapsing buildings and torn by flying glass. Others would fall victim to firestorms and fallout injuries. The latter injuries would include whole-body radiation injury; superficial radiation burns; and injuries produced by the deposition of radioactive substances within the body.[24]

Virtually all medical facilities and personnel would become inoperative. Those that might still exist would be taxed beyond endurance. Faced with victims suffering from multiple injuries, i.e., combinations of burn, blast, and radiation injuries, surviving physicians would inevitably resort to triage practice—a system for allocating medical resources in disaster conditions whereby the least injured and most injured receive no medical treatment.[25]

Complicating the critical inadequacy of postwar medical care would be unusable water supplies, disappearance of housing and shelter, and the complete breakdown of transportation and communication systems. Emergency police and fire services would be decimated, all systems of electrical power operation would cease functioning, and severe trauma would occasion widespread disorientation for which there would be no available therapy.

Normal society would be a thing of the past: the pestilence of wanton murder and banditry would exacerbate the presence of plague and epidemics. With the passage of time, many of the survivors would fall victim to degenerative diseases and various forms of cancer. And they might also expect premature death, impaired vision, and an increased probability of sterility.

Aristotle, in his *Poetics,* maintains that the playgoer, upon witnessing a great tragedy, undergoes a purgation of soul, a catharsis, out of pity and terror for the characters' and his own lot. In the years ahead, we are all likely to become involuntary playgoers at a performance in the absurd theater of contemporary international life. This performance could take place anywhere in the world, and would involve the enactment of nuclear terrorism in any of its myriad forms. Through the miracle of today's instantaneous communications technology, virtually all of the inhabitants of this endangered planet would be riveted to the stage.

It is doubtful, however, that many of us would experience the kind of catharsis described by Aristotle. Rather, our sentiments, for the most part, would be markedly one-sided, with little or no concern for the fate of the performers. The truest catharsis, ironically enough, would almost certainly be felt by the actors, whose very purpose in performing would be the need for spectacular self-assertion. Imbued with devotion to the "creativity" of violence, their drama would act out the ritualistic urgings of destructive passion. At the final curtain, the players would celebrate their liberation of irrepressible violence.

But the play doesn't have to end this way. In fact, it need not be performed at all. Bertolt Brecht, whose critical writing on the theater has had a profound effect on twentieth-century drama, once remarked that the actor performs according to the wishes of the audience. Indeed, says Brecht, "he is entirely dependent on the audience, blindly subject to it."[26] Understood in terms of the prospect of nuclear terrorism, Brecht's wisdom suggests a compelling need for more general awareness of what could happen, a far-reaching lucidity that uncovers terrible possibilities and produces alternate cues.

Part 2

Preventing Nuclear Terrorism

Introduction

The utopianizing of Robert Owen, the nineteenth-century Welsh reformer, inspired the following lines of the poem "New Harmony" by Adrien Stoutenberg:

> All that was needed was a plan
> to build a terrestrial paradise
> where men, not angels, could convene
> around the circular throne of hope.

We, too, need such a "plan," not for a "terrestrial paradise," but for avoiding the maelstrom of unplumbed depths threatened by nuclear terrorism. Without such a plan to snatch us from the hazardous flux of an absurd world politics, hope could give way to the silent completeness of a desolated planet.

Of course, we may, as a species, fall victim to such an apocalyptic end anyway. A number of present-day cosmologists believe that the universe exhibits neither point nor purpose, but is merely an infinitely repeating series of accidental bounces. In contrast to the Biblical version of creation, this model describes a "closed" universe, one that explodes, expands, falls back on itself, and explodes again, eternally. It means, in short, that the universe undergoes infinite reconstitution, and that every event undergoes eternal recurrence. If this model were correct, then there would really be no reason to search for a "plan." The pointlessness of the closed universe would ensure the pointlessness of reformist hopes.

But we really don't know if the universe is "open" or "closed," and it would surely be prudent—in the absence of a persuasive master theory—to assume the singularity of an explosive genesis and of subsequent human events. To assume otherwise would be to make certain that what might not have been fated would nevertheless take place through inaction. In this regard, we would do well to heed the words of the Chorus in Swiss dramatist Max Frisch's play, *The Firebugs:*

> Just because it happened,
> Don't put the blame on God,
> Nor on our human nature,
> Nor on our fruitful earth,
> Nor on our radiant sun. . . .
> Just because it happened,
> Must you call the damned thing Fate?

We must act! It would be folly to accept the ebbing of planetary life with autumnal resignation. We *do* need a plan. And we must heighten the consciousness of general publics throughout the world to this need.

This plan must be more than the usual commitment to a mélange of laws, treaties, and safeguards. Of course, such modalities of counterterrorist strategy are essential to the avoidance of nuclear catastrophe, and they will be carefully developed in the following three chapters. But they are not enough. What is also needed, and what must inform the entire configuration of technical/legal/political/military remedies, is an entirely new orientation to international political life. This orientation must replace the existing separation of conflictual nations from the global community with a new understanding of the benefits of interrelatedness.

The states in world politics must begin to fashion their foreign policies on a new set of premises, one that defines national interest in terms of what is best for the world system as a whole. By supplanting competitive self-seeking with cooperative self-seeking, and by renouncing the "everyone for himself" principle in world affairs, states can begin to move away from the social-Darwinian ethic that would otherwise assure our oblivion. By building upon the understanding that it is in each state's best interests to develop foreign policy from a systemic vantage point, and by defining national interests in terms of strategies that secure and sustain the entire system of states, our national leaders can begin to match the awesome agenda of world order reform with effective strategies of response. With such a starting point, the prevention of global nuclear catastrophe could draw its animating vision from the wisdom of Pierre Teilhard de Chardin: "The egocentric ideal of a future reserved for those who have managed to attain egoistically the extremity of 'everyone for himself' is false and against nature. No element could move and grow except with and by all the others with itself."

The false communion of nation-states is inwardly rotten, time-dishonored, close to collapsing. A communion based on fear and dread, its mighty efforts at producing increasingly destructive weapons have occasioned a deep desolation of the human spirit. The world has conquered technology only to lose its soul.

"The world, as it is now," Herman Hesse once wrote about the first quarter of the present century, "wants to die, wants to perish—and it will." No doubt, were he alive today, Hesse would see no need to change that observation. Indeed, as an anticipatory vision of what lies ahead, it is more exquisitely attuned to the present moment than to its intended time. Recognizing this fact, the following chapters are conceived with a view to altering this vision, to rendering it inaccurate. To accomplish this, international *angst* must give way to community, and humanity's store of international ideals must yield a gentle and new harmony.

Hardening the Target: Physical Security and Nonproliferation

In Franz Kafka's terrifying novella, *The Metamorphosis*, Gregor Samsa— the central figure—awakes one morning to find himself transformed into a gigantic insect. Confronted by the awful realization that their son is vermin who must be shut out from the human circle, Gregor's parents evaluate different strategies for dealing with the strange creature. Frau Samsa, diagnosing her son's plight as illness, sends for the doctor. But Herr Samsa, seeing only hostility and disobedience in Gregor's condition, sends for the locksmith. Gregor himself is heartened by both calls for help, and remarks that he cannot really distinguish between the role of the doctor and that of the locksmith.

This story is pertinent to our concern with preventing nuclear terrorism because we, too, must decide between the "doctor" and the "locksmith," between changing the condition of the terrorist "pathology" or placing new "locks" on the terrorist potential for violence. To date, the locksmith has been far more popular than the doctor. Defining the threat in physical security terms, governments have consistently focused their attention and resources on the search for a mechanical/technological fix. As a result, the prevention of nuclear terrorism continues to be characterized by an all-consuming preoccupation with guards, firearms, fences, and space-age protection devices.

Of course, if the "locksmith" is to be truly helpful in preventing nuclear terrorism, physical security measures will have to be implemented internationally. In this connection, special efforts must be made to ensure the success of the nonproliferation regime and to encourage international acceptance of International Atomic Energy Agency (IAEA) security standards. Until access to nuclear fuel and assembled nuclear weapons is prevented on a worldwide basis, unilateral measures will be inadequate.

Preventing Nuclear Terrorism Through Improved Physical Security

To prevent nuclear terrorism, physical barriers must be established that block access to strategic special nuclear materials and nuclear weapons. With this in mind, a growing counter-nuclear-terrorism technology is now being developed. This technology, which is designed to raise the prospective costs of "going nuclear," includes guard forces, fences, sensors, closed-circuit televisions, metal detectors, tags for explosives, and secure communications links.[1]

In the United States, the protection of nuclear materials is the responsibility of the Department of Energy and the Nuclear Regulatory Commission. According to a report issued by the General Accounting Office—"Commercial Nuclear Fuel Facilities Need Better Security"—there are differences between the two programs. The report mentions differences in instructions to guards concerning the use of force, the application of personnel screening programs, and the pace of upgrading in safeguards programs.[2]

To ensure a high level of protection for strategic special nuclear materials and nuclear reactors, the Nuclear Regulatory Commission—whose criteria for safeguards adequacy have elicited the greater share of criticism[3]—is now engaged in additional safeguards projects. These projects include a new guard-training upgrade rule (for fuel cycle facilities, transportation activities, and power reactors), increased protection for SSNM shipments and certain nonpower reactors, and a more clearly codified set of classification standards for use in the safeguards area.[4] In connection with its concern for the safeguard of nuclear materials against malevolent action during interfacility transport, the Nuclear Regulatory Commission has been seeking to develop an integrated system of conceptual design requirements.[5]

While such efforts at sound physical security are far from perfect, they do define the kinds of strategies that need to be replicated on a global basis.

With reference to the protection of assembled nuclear weapons, responsibility in the United States rests with the Department of Defense. Thus far, it appears that in terms of relative protection, DOD standards for nuclear weapons are of a higher order than DOE/NRC standards for SSNM.[6] Moreover, from the standpoint of effective worldwide standards for nuclear weapons, it appears that the most promising course would involve widespread imitation and replication of those measures and procedures developed by the DOD.

These measures and procedures, which are continually being upgraded and scrutinized, include a Permissive Action Link (PAL) program, which consists of "a code system and a family of devices integral or attached to nuclear weapons that have been developed to reduce the probability of an unauthorized nuclear detonation"; a Personnel Reliability Program (PRP), which consists of a continual screening and evaluation of nuclear duty personnel to assure reliability; a series of storage area classifications that delineate viable zones of protection; an Intrusion Detection Alarm (IDA) system; security forces capable of withstanding and repelling seizure efforts by terrorists; two-man concept control during any operation that may afford access to nuclear weapons, whereby "a minimum of two (2) authorized personnel, each capable of detecting incorrect or unauthorized procedures with respect to the task to be performed and familiar with applicable safety and security requirements, shall be present"; counterintelligence and investigative services, to actively seek information concerning threats to nuclear weapons; and carefully worked out logistic movement procedures, to ensure nuclear weapons security in transit.[7]

Preventing Nuclear Terrorism Through Nonproliferation

The present nonproliferation regime is based upon a series of multilateral agreements, statutes, and safeguards. The principal elements of this series are the Atomic Energy Act of 1954; the Statute of the International Atomic Energy Agency, which came into force in 1957; the Nuclear Test Ban Treaty, which entered into force on October 10, 1963; the Outer Space Treaty, which entered into force on October 10, 1967; the Treaty for the Prohibition of Nuclear Weapons in Latin America, which entered into force on April 22, 1968; and the Seabeds Arms Control Treaty, which entered into force on May 18, 1972.

The single most important element of the nonproliferation regime, however, is the Treaty on the Non-Proliferation of Nuclear Weapons, which entered into force on March 5, 1970. Since Article 6 of this treaty calls for an end to the nuclear arms race between the superpowers,[8] the SALT treaties and negotiations must also be counted as part of the nonproliferation regime. Before the world's nonnuclear powers can begin to take nonproliferation seriously, the United States and the Soviet Union will have to take prompt steps to bring their nuclear armaments under control. At the United Nations Special Session on Disarmament in 1978, there was a great deal of disenchantment about the fact that the two nuclear superpowers had not yet given meaningful content to that pledge.

In the view of the nonnuclear-weapons states, a "bargain" has been struck between the superpowers and themselves. Unless the Soviet Union and the United States begin to take more ambitious steps toward implementation of the Article 6 pledge, they, too, will move in the direction of nuclear capability. The nonnuclear powers consider this bargain the most prudential path to safety.

From the standpoint of controlling nuclear proliferation and preventing nuclear terrorism, this suggests that the superpowers must restructure their central strategic relationship. Such restructuring must be oriented toward a return to strategies of "minimum deterrence," a comprehensive nuclear test ban; a joint renunciation of first use of nuclear weapons; and a joint effort toward creating additional nuclear-weapon–free zones.

Minimum Deterrence

First the United States and the Soviet Union must return to the relative sanity of strategies based upon the ability to inflict overwhelming damage upon the aggressor after absorbing a nuclear first strike. It is widely understood that each side now has far more weaponry than is necessary for minimum deterrence. Since the survival of even the smallest fraction of U.S. or Soviet ICBMs, bombers, and submarines could assure the destruction of the other, we now have fantastic levels of overkill. No conceivable breakthrough in military technology can upset either side's minimum deterrence capability.

Within the structure of SALT deliberations, the return to minimum deterrence must involve more than a treaty based on Vladivostok guidelines. Most importantly, it must involve major commitments to further strategic weapons reductions, more comprehensive qualitative constraints on new strategic weapon systems, and provisions for improved verification.

Comprehensive Test Ban

Second, the time has come for a banning of all nuclear weapons testing. Despite the 1963 Partial Test Ban Treaty, the 1973 Limited Test Ban Treaty, the 1974 Treaty on the Limitation of Underground Nuclear Weapon Tests, the 1974 Threshold Treaty, the 1976 Treaty on Underground Nuclear Explosions for Peaceful Purposes, and the SALT II protocol provision dealing with flight testing of ICBMs, new types of ballistic missiles, and certain kinds of cruise missiles, only a comprehensive test ban can substantially inhibit further nuclear-weapons innovations. Now the subject of a major joint U.S.-Soviet working group, a comprehensive nuclear test ban would

represent the fulfillment of a goal first outlined in the late
1950s.

Both superpowers are on record in favor of a Comprehensive
Test Ban (CTB). President Carter has made such a ban a principal objective of his overall plan for arms control and disarmament. He announced his intentions on this issue before the
United Nations on March 17, 1977, and on October 4, 1977,
when he told the General Assembly, "The time has come to end
all explosions of nuclear devices, no matter what their claimed
justification, peaceful or military."[9]

No-First-Use Pledge

Third, the superpowers must take the declaratory step of
renouncing first use of nuclear weapons. Regrettably, while a
no-first-use pledge would be an important first step in the
process of "de-legitimizing" nuclear weapons, the United States
continues to oppose such a measure. This opposition stems
from the NATO strategy of deterring Soviet conventional attack with U.S. nuclear weapons. U.S. policy excludes the use
of nuclear weapons as the first offensive move of war (a first
strike), but does not exclude their retaliatory use to stave off
defeat in a major conventional conflict.

It is clear from present policy that a no-first-use pledge would
be contrary to the rudiments of U.S. nuclear deterrence strategy.
To permit a renunciation of the first-use option, the United
States would have to calculate that the expected benefits of
such renunciation would outweigh the expected costs. To allow
such a calculation, which would involve abandonment of the
neutron bomb, redeployment of theater nuclear forces away
from frontiers, and ultimate removal of these forces altogether,
the United States would have to undertake substantial efforts
to upgrade conventional forces. These efforts would be needed
to preserve a sufficiently high nuclear threshold.

Nuclear-Weapon-Free Zones

Fourth, the superpowers must augment their no-first-use

pledge with an effective plan for nuclear-free zones. The concept of such zones has already received international legal expression in the Treaty for the Prohibition of Nuclear Weapons in Latin America (the Treaty of Tlatelolco), which entered into force on April 22, 1968, and the two protocols to the treaty. Unlike two earlier treaties that seek to limit the spread of nuclear weapons into "pristine" areas—the Antarctic Treaty of 1961 and the Outer Space Treaty of 1967—the Latin American treaty concerns a populated area. The terms of the treaty include measures to prevent the type of deployment of nuclear weapons that led to the Cuban missile crisis, methods of verification by both the parties themselves and by their own regional organization, and IAEA safeguards on all nuclear materials and facilities under the jurisdiction of the parties.

In the years ahead, the Treaty of Tlatelolco must become a model for imitation in other areas of the world. In the absence of far-reaching respect for NPT (nonproliferation treaty) commitments, nuclear-weapon-free zones offer an auspicious means of reducing the number of sources of superpower confrontation and conflict. A majority of states already supports the idea of nuclear-weapon-free zones.

We have seen that the superpowers, by restructuring their central strategic relationship along the lines of minimum deterrence, comprehensive test ban, no-first-use pledges, and nuclear-weapon-free zones, could offer the nonnuclear-weapons states a significant incentive not to proliferate. Additional incentives, however, would also be needed. Of these, the most important would be an understanding that nuclear weapons do not enhance the security of those states that still do not possess them. While such a view would prove difficult to understand in a world committed to the principles of "realism," its essential truthfulness suggests some cause for optimism. This cause might be heightened by maintaining the burdensome costs associated with a military nuclear program and by offering superpower security assurances to nonnuclear allies.

The nuclear powers might also contribute to the cause of

nonproliferation with a pledge not to use nuclear weapons against nonweapon states.[10] Such a pledge, if it were generally credible, could contribute to the understanding that non-aquisition of nuclear weapons promotes safety. For example, accession to such a pledge by Israel, a "near-nuclear" power, might provide incentives to certain Arab states not to "go nuclear."

In conjunction with these measures, the IAEA must be granted greater authority to inspect nuclear facilities, search for clandestine stockpiles, and pursue stolen nuclear materials. Ultimately, such authority must be extended to all nuclear facilities of all nonnuclear-weapons states. Without such a tightening of IAEA safeguards, a number of nonnuclear-weapons states can be expected to calculate that the benefits of nonproliferation are exceeded by the costs.

International Atomic Energy Agency safeguards might also be tightened by the implementation of regional or multinational fuel-cycle centers. The rationale of such an arrangement, which was given considerable endorsement at the NPT Review Conference in May 1975, is that nations within a particular region would use a single reprocessing plant. By removing the excuse for some states to build their own nuclear fuel reprocessing plants, such centers could define a promising new approach to the problem of plutonium diversion. The resultant reduction of proliferation risks associated with sensitive fuel cycle activities could significantly reduce the likelihood of nuclear terrorism.

The strengthening and expanding of IAEA safeguards and functions is essential to nonproliferation and the avoidance of nuclear terrorism. These goals can also be served by an improved international capability for gathering covert intelligence. In the future, many of the intelligence capabilities that now rest entirely with national governments will need to be pooled and coordinated.[11]

A final arena in which the nonproliferation regime can be improved is that of nuclear export policy. This is the case because access to a nuclear weapons capability now depends largely on the policies of a small group of supplier states. In the years ahead, these states—which carry on international commerce in nuclear facilities, nuclear technology, and nuclear materials—will have to improve and coordinate their export policies.

The crux of the problem is the duality of nuclear exports. Although they contribute to the spread of nuclear weapons, they are also an exceptionally lucrative market for the supplier states. Therefore, unless every supplier state can be convinced that its own commitment to restraint in the export of sensitive technologies will be paralleled by every other supplier state, the hazards of a worldwide plutonium economy will be irrepressible.

To avert these hazards, two systems are required: (1) a system for verification of compliance with common nuclear export policies; and (2) a system of sanctions for noncompliance in which the costs of departure from such policies are so great as to outweigh the anticipated benefits of export revenues. Without such systems, the obligations on nuclear exports now imposed by IAEA, Euratom, and the NPT will have no meaningful effect.

In the control of nuclear exports, sanctions can play a vital part in affecting the decisions of recipient states. Since nonproliferation is an integral part of the plan to prevent nuclear terrorism, such sanctions must be considered to be targeted against states that support or at least tolerate the prospect of such terrorism. In this connection, such sanctions are already a part of this country's agreements for nuclear cooperation with certain other countries; the IAEA statute; and the Foreign Assistance Act as amended by the International Assistance and Arms Export Control Act of 1976. The specific sanctions in these cases include suspension of agreements and the return of transferred materials; curtailment or suspension of assistance provided by the IAEA; suspension from membership in the IAEA; and ineligibility for economic, military, or security assistance.[12]

Nonproliferation and International Political Power

Ultimately, the effectiveness of nonproliferation as a means to prevent nuclear terrorism will depend upon a cooperative effort by the United States and the Soviet Union to control limited aspects of their respective alliance systems. Moreover, it will depend upon an extension of such superpower control to all prospective proliferator states that fall under the orbit of U.S. or Soviet influence. While such a statement seems to exhibit characteristics of a new elitism, the effect of such control would be to bolster world order rather than primacy. Rather than reassert an earlier form of duopolistic domination, a selective tightening of bipolarity in world power processes could significantly enhance the promise of nonproliferation. This is the case because a tightening of superpower control over allies and other states would limit the freedom of action these states have to "go nuclear." The "tighter" the dualism of power, the greater the ability of the superpowers to assure broad compliance with nonproliferation goals and thereby prevent nuclear terrorism.

An important part of the nonproliferation/nuclear terrorism problem, therefore, is the control of too large a number of independent national wills. Such control is an instance of the more general problem of decision that arises when the benefits of common action are contingent upon the expectation that all parties will cooperate. Nonproliferation efforts will always be problematic to the extent that they rely upon volitional compliance. They may, however, be successful if the superpowers move with determination to assure the compliance of other states with the NPT and its associated norms and restrictions.

Not long ago, a letter to the Editor of the *New York Times* suggested a novel way to deal with the hazards of nuclear proliferation—the establishment of a new state, Neutronia, wherein those who choose to fight can unleash their aggressions without harm to citizens of other states. Here, says the writer, the world's generals could combat-ready volunteer troops, strategies could check-out tactics, officers could gain the front-line experience so necessary for promotions. Terrorists could carry submachine guns even at dinner parties, choosing lots to be the unfortunate schoolchild or tourist of the evening. Officials—prestigious and petty, righteous and corrupt—could plot and plunder, muggers could mug, thugs could waylay and torture. Here David Berkowitz could have killed Lila Kaled instead of Stacy Moscowitz. If Amin or Aman, the Politburo or the National Security Council ever felt like having a war, they would know where they could go.[13]

It is an interesting thesis. But it rests upon the mistaken assumption (even though it is obviously meant as satire, and not as a serious proposal) that the dangers of nuclear catastrophe in world politics stem from the presence of a "tiny minority" with base instincts. The problem, the letter implies, is that the inclination to carry out cataclysmic conflict is simply our individual murderous instincts writ large. It follows that by separating the murderous from the peaceful, the bad from the good, the vast majority of our species could "raise our glasses" to one more flag at the United Nations and "get on with the business of living."[14]

If only it were really that simple. The fact of the matter is that the impending spread of nuclear weapons is fueled not by madness or malignant motives, but by basically well-intentioned persons who find such weapons essential to "national security." To prevent the spread of such weapons, therefore, we must not seek to root out the bad from the good, but to convince everyone that "going nuclear" would be counterproductive.

In principle, this should not be difficult to do. As we have already seen, no strategy for security could possibly be less realistic than what is called "realism." Nonetheless, old ideas, however time dishonored, do not die easily, and the creation of a new system of world security will require a species of fortitude that borders on the sublime.

To begin, the scaffolding of the present nonproliferation

regime will have to be strengthened by a restructuring of the central strategic relationship of the superpowers; an improved nonproliferation treaty; the implementation of regional or multinational nuclear fuel cycle centers; the strengthening of IAEA safeguards and functions; the expansion of nuclear-free zones; and common and effective nuclear export policies. After this scaffolding has been firmed up, it will be necessary for the superpowers to cooperate more self-consciously in pursuit of nonproliferation goals. At a critical juncture during such cooperation, the Soviet Union and the United States will have to extend their own previously worked-out principles of nuclear war avoidance to the rest of the family of nations. These principles, of course, will rest on a new understanding of national interests—one that recognizes the futility of military competition and the imperative of working for the survival of the system as a whole.

Will it work? Can humankind be expected to grasp hold of this calculus of potentiality, reaffirming the sovereignty of reason over the forces of disintegration? Can nations be expected to tear down the walls of competitive power struggles and replace them with the permeable membranes of spirited cooperation?

Probably not! But there is surely no other way. So long as individual states continue to identify their own security with the acquisition of destructive weaponry they will have only war. The Talmud tells us, "The dust from which the first man was made was gathered in all the corners of the world." By moving toward a new planetary identity, the peoples of earth can begin to build bridges over the most dangerous abyss they have ever known. Hopefully, even in this absurd theater of modern world politics, human beings will choose life rather than death. Stripped of false hopes, and without illusion, man may yet stare at the specter of nuclear holocaust with passionate attention, and experience the planetary responsibility that will bring liberation.

We began this inquiry into strategies of counternuclear terrorism with a brief synopsis of Kafka's novella, *The Metamorphosis.* The story is pertinent to our concerns as a parable that illustrates the options at hand: (1) summoning the locksmith (improved physical security) and (2) sending for the doctor (improved behavioral measures). Both options must be pursued vigorously, imaginatively, internationally, and simultaneously.

At the moment, however, only the first option is being taken seriously. The second continues to be widely ignored. This situation is as absurd as the literary genre that springs from Kafka's oblique way of regarding experience. To reach and sustain a more hopeful situation, one in which the human race is granted a functional dispensation from nuclear terrorism, nations will have to place ever greater emphasis on behavioral countermeasures.

Internationally, as we shall now see, such measures must include special patterns of cooperation between like-minded governments; sanctions against states that sponsor or support terrorism; and a fuller application of international legal norms. With respect to international law, greater respect must be accorded to the principle of "extradite or prosecute"; states must broaden the definition of aggression approved by the General Assembly in 1974; and terrorists must come to be regarded by all states as "common enemies of mankind." Taken together, such measures could severely limit the likelihood of nuclear terrorism.

However, to be genuinely promising, such measures will require a far more sweeping transformation of world politics, one in which all states renounce mindless "realism" in favor of planetary consciousness. To begin this transformation, states must arrive at the understanding that fostering terrorism can never be in their long-term best interests. The unity of states against terrorism is the essential precondition for avoiding terrorist nuclear violence. Such unity, therefore, is also an essential requirement of a secure world order.

A few years after the Declaration of Independence, the Continental Congress adopted as a motto on the Great Seal of the United States a phrase of Virgil's, *Novus Ordo Seclorum* ("a new age beginning"). In a world imperilled by multiple dangers of nuclear violence, it is time for such a motto to be applied internationally. Nuclear terrorism, like the other principal paths to nuclear catastrophe in world politics, is threatening largely because of the uninterrupted primacy of militaristic nationalism among states. Its terrible possibilities, including nuclear war, can be avoided only when states escape from their own misconceptions of self-interest. To witness a new age beginning among all states, citizens of the world must work to remove these misconceptions, substituting the dignity of cooperation for the degradation of mortal competition. In so doing, they can create an intellectual and spiritual foundation upon which the move to planetization can be actualized.

5

Softening the Adversary:
Behavioral Strategies

Even if sophisticated physical security measures are extended throughout the world, they will not be adequate for the task at hand. It is not enough to safeguard strategic special nuclear materials and nuclear weapons to prevent nuclear terrorism. To augment physical safeguards, we must create a *behavioral* strategy, one that is directed toward producing certain changes in the decisional calculi of terrorist groups and their sponsor states.

Such a behavioral strategy must be based upon a sound understanding of the risk calculations of terrorists. Until we understand the special terrorist stance on the balance of risks that can be taken in world politics, we will not be able to identify an appropriate system of sanctions. Although terrorists are typically apt to tolerate higher levels of death and injury than states, there *is* a threshold beyond which certain costs become intolerable.

To understand this threshold, we must first recall that there is no such thing as "the terrorist mind." Rather, there are a great many terrorist minds, an almost unbelievable potpourri of ideas, methods, visions, and objectives. To seek a uniformly applicable strategy of counternuclear terrorism, therefore, would represent the height of folly.

Contrariwise, in spite of the obvious heterogeneity that characterizes modern terrorism, it would be immensely impractical to formulate myriad different strategies that are tailored to particular groups. What must be established is a limited and manageable number of basic strategies that are formed according to the principal types of terrorist group behavior. By adopting this means of "blueprinting" effective counternuclear terrorist action, policy makers can be presented with a decision-making taxonomy in which strategies are differentiated according to the particular category of risk calculation involved.

This is not to suggest that each terrorist group is comprised of individuals who exhibit the same pattern of behavior, i.e., the same stance on the balance of risks that can be taken in pursuit of particular preferences. Rather, each terrorist group is made up, in varying degrees, of persons with disparate motives. Since it is essential, from the point of view of creating the necessary decisional taxonomy, that each terrorist *group* be categorized according to a particular type of risk calculation, the "trick" is to identify and evaluate the leadership strata of each terrorist group in order to determine the predominant ordering of preferences.

In terms of actually mounting an effective counternuclear terrorist strategy, therefore, governments must organize their activities according to the following sequence of responsibilities:

1. Appraise the terrorist group under scrutiny for the purpose of identifying leadership elements.
2. Appraise the leadership elements for the purpose of identifying predominant patterns of risk-calculation.
3. Examine the decision-making taxonomy for the purpose of identifying the appropriate type of counternuclear terrorist strategy, i.e., the strategy that corresponds with the identified pattern of risk calculation.

In so organizing their counternuclear terrorist activities, governments can begin to develop a rationally conceived "behavioral technology" that distinguishes contingencies of reinforcement according to the particular type of terrorists involved. To deal effectively with the prospective problem of nuclear terrorism, it is essential to correlate deterrent and remedial measures with the preference orderings and modus operandi of the particular terrorist group(s) in question.

Examples of the Theory

For example, if a terrorist group displaying the self-sacrificing value system of *fedayeen* were to threaten nuclear violence, it would be inappropriate to base deterrence on threats of physically punishing acts of retaliation. Here, negative physical sanctions, unless they are devastating enough to ensure destruction of the group itself, are bound to be ineffective. Indeed, such sanctions might even have the effect of a *stimulus.* Instead of orthodox threats of punishment, deterrence in this case should be based upon threats that promise to obstruct preferences that the terrorist group values even more highly than physical safety.[1]

Such threats, therefore, should be directed at convincing terrorists that the resort to nuclear violence would mitigate against their political objectives. To support such threats, steps would probably have to be taken to convince the terrorists that higher-order acts of violence are apt to generate broad-based repulsion rather than support.[2] As long as the threatened act of nuclear violence stems from propagandistic motives, terrorists who associate such violence with unfavorable publicity may be inclined to less violent strategies.

Deterrence in this case might also be based upon the promise of rewards. Such a strategy of "positive sanctions" has been left out of current studies of counterterrorism; yet, it may prove to be one of the few potentially worthwhile ways of affecting the decisional calculi of terrorist groups with self-sacrificing value systems.[3] Of course, in considering whether this sort of strategy is appropriate in particular situations, governments will have to decide whether the expected benefits that accrue from avoiding nuclear terrorism are great enough to outweigh the prospective costs associated with the promised concessions.[4]

The reasonablesness of such a strategy is also enhanced by its probable long-term systemic effects. Just as violence tends to beget more violence,[5] rewards tend to generate more rewards. By the incremental replacement of negative sanctions with positive ones, a growing number of actors in world politics, terrorists as well as states, are apt to become habituated to the ideology of a reward system and to disengage from the dynamics of a threat or punishment system. The cumulative effect of such habituation is likely to be a more peaceful and harmonious world and national system, since there is no limit to the number of rewards that can be bestowed.[6]

For another example, we may consider the case of a terrorist group that exhibits a preference ordering very much like that of an ordinary criminal band, i.e., its actions are dictated largely by incentives of material gain, however much these incentives are rationalized in terms of political objectives.[7] If such a terrorist group were to threaten nuclear violence, it would be as inappropriate to base deterrence on threats of political failure or negative public reception as it would be to threaten self-sacrificing ideologues with personal harm. Rather, deterrence in this case should be based largely upon the kinds of threats that are used to counter orthodox criminality. Indeed, in dealing with this particular type of terrorist group, it is not only vital to recognize its particular resemblance to an ordinary criminal band, but to "broadcast" this resemblance throughout the political system.[8] Once such terrorists have been widely identified as ordinary criminals, the counternuclear terrorist effort can be eased considerably.[9]

This is not to suggest, however, that threats of physically punishing retaliation will always be productive in dealing with this type of terrorist group. Even though this particular type, unlike the self-sacrificing variety considered in the first example, is apt to value personal safety in its ordering of preferences, threats to impair this safety may be misconceived. Indeed, a great deal of sophisticated conceptual analysis and experimental evidence now seems to indicate that, in certain cases, the threat of physical punishment may actually prove counterproductive.[10] Contrary to the widely held conventional wisdom on the matter, taking a hard-line approach toward terrorists may only reinforce antagonism and intransigence. Recent experience indicates that physical retaliation against terrorists often causes only a shift in the selection of targets and a more protracted pattern of violence and aggression. The threat of physical punishment against terrorists is apt to generate high levels of anger that effectively raise the threshold of acceptable suffering. This is the case because anger can modify usual cost/benefit calculations, overriding the inhibitions ordinarily associated with anticipated punishment.

To this point, the discussion of negative sanctions has been limited to physical punishment. However, there is considerable evidence that *all kinds* of negative sanctions, economic as well as physical, stiffen rather than diminish terrorist resistance. Whatever the nature of negative sanctions, they appear to generate anger that causes terrorists to value retaliation (or counter-retaliation, whichever the case may be) more highly than the objectives that have given rise to terrorist activity in the first place.

For a third example, we may consider the case of a terrorist group that exhibits a primary concern for achieving one form or another of political objective, but that lacks the self-sacrificing value system of *fedayeen*.[11] If this sort of terrorist group were to threaten nuclear violence, it would be appropriate to base deterrence on a suitable combination of all of the negative and positive sanctions discussed thus far. This means that steps should be taken to convince the group that (1) nuclear violence would mitigate against its political objectives, (2) certain concessions would be granted in exchange for restraint from nuclear violence[12] and (3) certain physically punishing or otherwise negative acts of retaliation would be meted out if nuclear violence were undertaken.

In deciding upon what, exactly, constitutes a suitable configuration of sanctions, governments will have to be especially discriminating in their manner of brandishing threats of physical punishment. In this connection, it is worth noting that threats of mild punishment may have a greater deterrent effect than threats of severe punishment. From the vantage point of the terrorist group's particular baseline of expectations, such threats—when threats of severe punishment are expected—may even appear to have positive qualities. Catching the terrorist group by surprise, such threat behavior is also less likely to elicit the high levels of anger and intractability that tend to override the inhibiting factor of expected punishment.[13] Moreover, the threat of mild punishment is less likely to support the contention of official repression, a contention that is often a vital part of terrorist group strategies for success.[14]

In reference to the actual promise of rewards as an instrument of deterrence, governments may find it worthwhile to consider whether a selected number of particular concessions would produce a gainful net effect. In other words, recognizing that threats of severe punishment produce rationality-impairing stress, which in turn produces greater resistance rather than compliance, governments may discover that the promise of rewards communicates feelings of sympathy and concern, which in turn diminish terrorist resistance. With such an understanding, governments may begin to delimit the particular concessions which they are prepared to make.

A fourth and final example that illustrates the need to correlate deterrent and situational measures with particular preference orderings centers on the case of terrorist groups spurred on by the need for spectacular self-assertion. From the standpoint of preventing nuclear violence, this type of terrorist group presents the greatest problems. Faced with terrorist groups who long to act out the ritualistic urgings of Bakhunin, Sorel, Fanon, and Sartre, governments are confronted with genuine psychopaths and sociopaths. Clearly, since the preference that would need to be obstructed in this case is neither political success nor personal profit, but the violent act itself, and since personal safety is unlikely to figure importantly in the terrorist risk calculation, deterrence of nuclear terrorism must be abandoned altogether as a viable strategy. Instead, all preventive measures must concentrate upon limiting the influence of such terrorists within their particular groups and maintaining a safe distance between such terrorists and the instruments of higher-order weapons technologies.

If the apparent danger is great enough, governments may feel compelled to resort to a "no holds barred" counterterrorist campaign. In such cases, governments must be aware that the inclination to escalate violence would signify the erosion of power. As Hannah Arendt has pointed out, violence and power are opposites. Where the latter is in jeopardy, the former is increased.[15] Understood in terms of antiterrorism measures, this suggests that the imprudent escalation of violence by public authorities can destroy power. Taken to its outermost limits, such escalation can lead to rule by sheer violence and the substitution of "official" terror for insurgent terror.

The Problem of Civil Liberties

In the preceding examples, some of the prospective sanctions available to counternuclear terrorist strategists entail measures that might be injurious to such values as social justice and human rights within states. Of special interest in this connection are options involving:

1. A total, no-holds-barred military-type assault designed to eradicate the terrorist group(s) altogether; and/or
2. A protracted, counterterrorist campaign utilizing "classical" methods of informers, infiltrators, counterterrorist squads patterned, perhaps, after Israel's *Mivtah Elohim* ("God's wrath"), assassinations,[16] agents provocateurs, and selected raids.

The first option, however effective it might be, is apt to be most destructive of essential citizen rights. Hence, governments contemplating such an option must pay close attention to the necessary trade-off between efficacy and liberty that is involved. Since this option would almost certainly be repugnant to the most deeply held values of liberal, democratic societies, governments, before resorting to this option, would have to be convinced that its prospective benefits were great enough to outweigh its probable costs. In fact, short of its use at the situational level where higher-order acts of terrorist violence have already taken place, it is unlikely that this option will be taken seriously in democratic states. Rather, we are likely to see its adoption only by the world's most blatantly authoritarian, antidemocratic regimes.

This no-holds-barred military option is problematic for another reason. Not only might it incite fears of military/police repression among the more liberal sectors of the population, it might also confer a genuine combatant status upon the terrorists. As a result, the terrorist group(s) would more likely acquire the case of an underdog army than that of a criminal band.

The second option is also apt to score high marks on the efficacy dimension, but its effects on essential citizen rights need not be as injurious. This is not to suggest that a protracted counterterrorist campaign utilizing classical methods of apprehension and punishment would necessarily be any less repulsive to liberal, democratic societies, but that such a campaign might be conducted on a comparatively less visible and clandestine basis. An additional virtue of such quiet operations would be the avoidance of sympathy-generating publicity for the terrorist group(s).

In the final analysis, the problem of conflicting values that emerges from the consideration of harsh deterrent countermeasures can be resolved only by careful comparison of the costs and benefits involved.

In the absence of such a comparison, civil liberties might be curtailed under conditions far less threatening than nuclear terrorism. [17] A good example of this is Canadian Prime Minister Trudeau's response to *Front de Libération Quebecois* (FLQ) tactics of bombing and assassination in 1970. Taking steps to put his government on a genuine wartime footing against its internal insurgents, Trudeau invoked the War Measures Act on October 16, 1970, authorizing the government to do anything "it deems necessary for the security, defense, peace, order, and welfare of Canada." These steps were defended by the prime minister in his "total war" message to the country two days earlier:

> There are a lot of bleeding hearts around who just don't like to see people with helmets and guns. All I can say is, go on and bleed, but it is more important to keep law and order in the society than to be worried about weak-kneed people. . . . I think society must take every means at its disposal to defend itself against the emergence of a parallel power which defies the elected power in this country.

Canada is, of course, like the United States, a country that regards the protection of civil liberties as a fundamental principle of government. Yet, in 1970, in response to a relatively low-risk crisis situation, it adopted short-run measures so sweeping that they removed basic liberties from the citizenry.[18] It goes without saying, therefore, that the threat to civil liberties posed by nuclear terrorism in other, less democratic societies, is very real and must be taken seriously. In such societies, the line between underreaction and overreaction is unlikely to be walked with scrupulous concern.

In general, the optimal counternuclear terrorist strategy is one in which effective counteraction leaves the prevailing network of citizen rights and privileges unimpaired. Barring this possibility, however, the requirements of effective strategies[19] should be tempered by concern for those freedoms which are assured by humanitarian international law.[20]

In reference to the two options just outlined, it would be better from the civil-liberties point of view if their sanctioning methods could be replaced altogether by the use of positive sanctions; moderate, ad hoc acts of physical punishment; efforts at underscoring the orthodox criminality of terrorist activities; and sustained efforts to convince terrorists that higher-order violence would be counterproductive to their objectives. Indeed, it would surely be a good idea for counternuclear terrorist planners to begin to exploit the psychological warfare tactics that go back to the fifth century B.C. and Sun Tzu's *The Book of War.* Recognizing that in most cases, terrorist violence is not an end in itself, but an instrument for achieving desired personal/social/political change, certain terrorist groups might be deterred from nuclear violence to the extent that they believe such violence to be self-defeating. Unlike options 1 and 2, such tactics would recognize the primacy of ends over means in the preference orderings of most terrorist groups, and exploit this recognition by the establishment of reasoned countermeasures.

Such tactics, however, are intrinsically ill-suited to dealing with terrorist groups for whom higher-order acts of destruction are ends in themselves. In dealing with such groups, options 1 and 2 may circumscribe the government's only means of defending the citizens in its charge. It follows that in such cases, the exigencies of survival may have to take precedence over the claims of libertarian values.[21]

The Decision-Making Taxonomy

The following taxonomy identifies six principal types of terrorist groups and correlates each type with an appropriate strategy of deterrent and remedial measures. The six types are defined according to two principal factors: (1) degree of commitment to political objectives (high, moderate, or low) and (2) utilization of criminal (i.e., robbery or "expropriation" to secure funds) tactics (criminal or noncriminal).[22] Each type displays a distinctive stance on the balance of risks that can be taken in pursuit of particular preferences. It is up to responsible government officials to adapt this decision-making taxonomy to proper and necessary counternuclear terrorist efforts.

The Six Principal Types of Terrorist Groups

Table 1 lists the six principal types of terrorist groups. These types will be used in Table 2, the Decision-Making Taxonomy, which appears on page 92.

These six types range from what might be termed "pure altruism" (Type 1) to what comes very close to being "pure criminality" (Type 6). Psychopathic or nihilistic terrorism can fall under the heading of either Type 5 or Type 6.

Group Type 1

This type of terrorist group is characterized by a high degree of commitment to political objectives and an absence of criminal activity. Here, the self-sacrificing value system of *fedayeen* is in evidence, and the group does not secure needed funds through "expropriatory" activities. In view of the particular ordering of preferences associated with this type of terrorist group—an ordering that assigns much greater value to political objectives than to personal safety—deterrence efforts should focus upon threats to obstruct political objectives. Such threats must be directed at convincing the group that its resort to nuclear violence would mitigate against political objectives because it would both stiffen incumbent resolve and alienate vital bases of popular support. Deterrence might also be based upon a strategy of positive sanctions, in which certain rewards or concessions that relate to political objectives are promised in exchange for

Table 1   Six Principal Types of Terrorist Groups

Group Type	Degree of Commitment	Criminality
1	High	Noncriminal
2	High	Criminal
3	Moderate	Noncriminal
4	Moderate	Criminal
5	Low	Noncriminal
6	Low	Criminal

the nonuse of nuclear or higher-order weapons technologies. *Under no circumstances should deterrence of this type of terrorist group be based upon orthodox threats of physically punishing retaliation.*

Group Type 2

This type of terrorist group is characterized by a high degree of commitment to political objectives and by the utilization of criminal tactics. Here, the self-sacrificing value system of *fedayeen* is still in evidence, while the group secures needed funds through robberies of one kind or another. It follows that deterrence efforts should focus upon the same threats and promises associated with Group Type 1 *plus* efforts that exploit the criminal character of the group. This second category of efforts should concentrate upon creating a "bad press" for the group among potential adherents and supporters by spreading the news about the group's ordinary criminal tendencies.

Group Type 3

This type of terrorist group is characterized by a moderate degree of commitment to political objectives and by an absence of criminal activity. Here, the group's primary rationale and concern is still manifestly political, but there is no evidence of the self-sacrificing values. And the group does not secure funds through "expropriation." In view of the particular ordering of preferences associated with this type of terrorist group—an ordering that values both political objectives and personal safety—deterrence efforts should focus upon the same threats and promises associated with Group Type 1 *plus* an appropriate level of orthodox threats of physically punishing retaliation. Such negative sanctions are needed to compensate for the diminished (vis-à-vis Group Types 1 and 2) level of political commitment.

Group Type 4

This type of terrorist group is characterized by a moderate

degree of commitment to political objectives and by the utilization of criminal tactics. Here, the group's political concerns
mirror Group Type 3, but the group does secure funds through
robberies and holdups. It follows that deterrence efforts should
focus upon the same threats and promises associated with
Group Type 3 *plus* efforts to broadcast and publicize the group's
ordinary criminal activities. As in the case of deterrence efforts
associated with Group Type 2, such efforts are designed to alienate the group from vital bases of potential support.

Group Type 5

This type of terrorist group is characterized by a low degree
of commitment to political objectives and by the absence of
criminal activity. Here, the group's raison d'être is only nominal-
ly political, and the group does not secure funds through "expropriation." Typically, this type of group looks upon violence
as its own end rather than as an instrument. Moreover, violence
is viewed as a romantic and creative force that is self-justifying.
In view of the particular ordering of preferences associated with
this type of terrorist group—an ordering that values the violent
act itself more highly than any alleged political objectives—
deterrence should be abandoned altogether as a strategy of
counternuclear terrorism. Since such groups exhibit traits that
are best described as nihilistic or psychopathic, preventive
measures should focus upon "prophylaxis" via a counternuclear terrorism campaign that may or may not require preemption. And, since personal safety figures unimportantly in
this type of terrorist group's risk calculus, the application of
negative physical sanctions must be at the highest reasonable
levels, i.e., levels that are consistent with the society's basic
commitment to decency and essential human rights.

Group Type 6

This type of terrorist group is characterized by a low degree
of commitment to political objectives and by the use of criminal
tactics. Here, the group's nominal political concerns mirror

Table 2 The Decision-Making Taxonomy

Group Type	Group Characteristics	Counternuclear Terrorist Strategy
1	High degree of political commitment; no criminal activity. Self-sacrificing value system. Preference ordering assigns far greater value to political objectives than to personal safety.	Deterrence focused upon threats to obstruct political objectives and promises to assist with such objectives in exchange for nonuse of nuclear weaponry. No threats of physically punishing retaliation.
2	High degree of political commitment; use of criminal tactics. Self-sacrificing value system. Preference ordering assigns far greater value to political objectives than to personal safety.	Deterrence focused upon same threats and promised concessions as in Group Type 1 *plus* efforts to exploit criminal character of the group. These efforts to concentrate upon creating a "bad press."
3	Moderate degree of political commitment; no criminal activity No self-sacrificing value system. Preference ordering values both political objectives and personal safety.	Deterrence focused upon same threats and promises as in Group Type 1 *plus* an appropriate level of orthodox threats of physically punishing retaliation.
4	Moderate degree of political commitment; use of criminal tactics. Political concerns mirror Group Type 3.	Deterrence focused upon same threats and promises as in Group Type 3 *plus* efforts to publicize the group's ordinary criminal cast.
5	Low degree of political commitment; no criminal activity. Preference ordering values violence per se more highly than alleged political objectives. Group exhibits nihilistic/psychopathic traits.	Deterrence abandoned in favor of "prophylactic" preventive measures. Negative physical sanctions must be applied at highest reasonable levels. Waging of counternuclear terrorist campaign.
6	Low degree of political commitment; use of criminal tactics. Political concerns mirror Group Type 5. Group exhibits primary characteristics of bandit band; may also exhibit nihilistic/psychopathic traits as in Group Type 5.	Deterrence focused upon kinds of threats used against ordinary criminality *plus* preventive measures associated with Group Type 5.

Note: In all strategies involving positive sanctions, concessions should be based upon a predetermined (i.e., preincident) hierarchy of concessions rather than upon an ad hoc judgment of what can be allowed.

those of Group Type 5, but the group does secure funds through "expropriation." While this type of terrorist group may also exhibit nihilistic or psychopathic traits, its primary characteristics come closer to those of ordinary criminals or bandits. It follows that deterrence efforts should focus upon the kinds of threats that are used to counter orthodox criminality, and that these efforts must be augmented by the preventive measures associated with Group Type 5. The extent to which such preventive measures should be adopted depends largely on the extent to which the primary features of this type of terrorist group exhibit nihilistic/psychopathic rather than purely criminal traits.

Behavioral Measures at the International Level

Counternuclear terrorist strategies within states require differentiating sanctions according to the particular type of terrorist group involved. However, since nuclear terrorism might take place across national boundaries, the basic principles of these strategies must also be applied internationally. This means that those nations that are most vulnerable to nuclear terrorist attack must learn to call upon the "doctor" as well as the "locksmith." While it is critical for them to harden the target, it is also essential that they learn to soften the adversary. This means learning to understand the variety of terrorist-group preferences and the subtlety of ways in which these preferences can be exploited.

Of course, there are special difficulties involved in implementing behavioral measures of counternuclear terrorism internationally. These difficulties center on the fact that certain states sponsor and host terrorist groups and that such states extend the privileges of sovereignty to insurgents on their land. While it is true that international law forbids a state to allow its territory to be used as a base for aggressive operations against another state with which it is not at war,[23] a state that seeks to deal with terrorists hosted in another state is still in a very difficult position.

To cope with these difficulties, like-minded governments must create special patterns of international cooperation. These patterns must be based upon the idea that even sovereignty must yield to gross inversions of the norms expressed in the Charter of the United Nations; the Universal Declaration of Human Rights; the International Covenant on Economic, Social and Cultural Rights; the International Covenant on Civil and Political Rights; the Convention on the Prevention and Punishment of the Crime of Genocide; the European Convention for the Protection of Human Rights and Fundamental Freedoms; the American Convention on Human Rights; the Nuremberg principles; and the 1949 Geneva Conventions. They must, therefore, take the form of collective defense arrangements between particular states that promise protection and support for responsible acts of counternuclear terrorism.

Such arrangements must entail plans for cooperative intelligence gathering on the subject of terrorism and for exchange of the information produced; an expanded and refined tapestry of agreements on extradition of terrorists; multilateral forces to infiltrate terrorist organizations and, if necessary, to take action against them;[24] concerted use of the media to publicize terrorist activities and intentions; and counter-terrorism emergency medical networks. Such arrangements might also entail limited and particular acts directed toward effective counternuclear terrorism. Examples of such acts include the willingness of Kenya to allow Israeli planes refueling privileges during the Entebbe mission and the assistance of three ambassadors from Moslem states during the Hanafi Moslem siege of Washington, D.C., in March 1977.

Other arrangements might center on encouraging dissension among the various terrorist groups. Such arrangements would seem to be especially promising if applied to the various factions of the Palestinian movement. Internecine struggles within this movement have been obvious since the mid-1970s, when Arafat's PLO faction of Fatah, Al Saiqa, and PDFLP (Popular Democratic Front for the Liberation of Palestine) drew opposition from PFLP (Popular Front for the Liberation of Palestine), ALF (Arab Liberation Front), and PFLP—GC (Popular Front for the Liberation of Palestine—General Command) "rejectionists."

Above all else, however, international arrangements for counternuclear terrorist cooperation must include sanctions for states that sponsor or support terrorist groups and activities.[25] As in the case of sanctions applied to terrorists, such sanctions may include carrots as well as sticks. Until every state in the world system calculates that support of counternuclear terrorist measures is in its own interests, individual terrorist groups will have reason and opportunity to escalate their violent excursions.

In the United States, a provision to sanction states supporting international terrorism is included in the Omnibus Antiterrorism Act of 1979. Sections 105 and 106 of this bill (S. 333), which is intended to effect certain reorganization of the federal government to strengthen federal programs and policies for combating international and domestic terrorism, state the following:

LIST OF STATES SUPPORTING INTERNATIONAL TERRORISM

Sec. 105. (a) Six months after the date of enactment of this Act and each year thereafter, the President shall consider which, if any, states have demonstrated a pattern of support for acts of international terrorism. If the President determines that any states have so acted, he shall submit a list of states supporting international terrorism to the President pro tempore of the Senate and the Speaker of the House of Representatives, and set forth his reasons for listing any such states. The President may at any time add to any such list the name of any state supporting international terrorism by transmitting the name of such state to the President pro tempore of the Senate and the Speaker of the House of Representatives together with his reasons for adding the name of such state to the list. If the President determines that no states have undertaken such acts, he shall report the same with a detailed explanation.

(b) Such list shall also identify any states against which sanctions have been applied pursuant to section 106 of this Act, and any other initiatives of the United States with respect to such states.

(c) Nothing in this section is intended to require the public disclosure of information which is properly classified under criteria established by

Executive order, or is otherwise protected by law. Such information shall be provided to the President pro tempore of the Senate and the Speaker of the House of Representatives in a written classified report. In such case, an unclassified summary of such information shall be prepared and submitted to the President pro tempore of the Senate and the Speaker of the House of Representatives.

(d) Nothing in this section is intended to require disclosure of investigatory records compiled for law enforcement purposes specifically protected by section 552(b)(7) of title 5, United States Code.

(e)(1) The list shall be reviewed periodically by the President. The President may propose to Congress a request for removal of any state from the list. Such request shall be accompanied by the reasons therefor.

(2) A state requested by the President to be deleted from the list shall be removed from the list thirty days after the submission of that request to the Congress unless Congress by concurrent resolution disapproves that request.

SANCTIONS AGAINST STATES SUPPORTING INTERNATIONAL TERRORISM

Sec. 106. (a) When a foreign government is listed pursuant to section 105 of this Act, the President shall—

(1) Provide no assistance under the Foreign Assistance Act of 1961, or

(2) not authorize any sale, or extend any credit or guaranty, with respect to any defense article or service as defined by section 47 of the Arms Export Control Act, or

(3) approve no export license for the export of commodities or technical data which would enhance the military potential of the foreign government or which would otherwise enhance its ability to support acts of international terrorism, or

(4) extend no duty-free treatment under title V of the Trade Act of 1974, or

(5) permit no entry to the United States by nationals of such country, or foreign nationals sponsored by such country, for the purpose of acquiring training or education in nuclear sciences or subjects having military applicability.

(b)(1) If the President finds that the interests of national security so require, he may suspend the applicability of all or any part of the prohibitions listed in subsection (a) of this section in such case: *Provided,* That the President consults with the appropriate committees of Congress prior to the suspension of such prohibitions. He shall report his reasons therefor in writing in detail to the President pro tempore of the Senate, and the Speaker of the House of Representatives and those prohibitions shall not apply.

(2) In determining which of the prohibitions in subsection (a) of this section should be taken, the President, in consultation with Congress, shall consider—

(A) the effectiveness of suspending any prohibition in inducing change in a country's policy or practice of supporting acts of international terrorism;

(B) the effect of such suspension on United States relations with other governments; and

(C) the effects of such suspension on other national interests of the United States.

(c) In devising initiatives to combat international terrorist actions and to reduce state support for such actions, the President shall take such other measures available to him as he deems appropriate; he shall take into account the effectiveness of specific sanctions in inducing change in a country's policy or practice of supporting acts of international terrorism; the likely effect of sanctions on overall United States relations with such country or with other countries; and the effect such sanctions would have on other United States national interests.

(d) The President shall take all appropriate diplomatic measures consistent with international obligations to support the effectiveness of actions taken pursuant to this authority in the accomplishment of the purposes of this Act.

(e) The President shall promptly and fully inform the President pro tempore of the Senate and the Speaker of the House of Representatives of each exercise of authority granted under the Act.

(f) Nothing in this section is intended to require the public disclosure of information that is properly classified under criteria established by Executive order or is otherwise protected by law. Such information shall be provided to the President pro tempore of the Senate and to the Speaker of the House of Representatives in a written classified report. In such case, an unclassified summary of such information shall be prepared and submitted to the President pro tempore of the Senate and the Speaker of the House of Representatives.

Additional Measures Under International Law

The international legal order has tried to cope with transnational terrorism since 1937, when the League of Nations produced two conventions to deal with the problem. These conventions proscribed acts of terror-violence against public officials, criminalized the impairment of property and the infliction of general injuries by citizens of one state against those of another, and sought to create an international criminal court with jurisdiction over terrorist crimes. The advent of the Second World War, however, prevented the ratification of either document.[26]

An international criminal court[27] is, however, unlikely to come into being. But there are other measures under international law that could and should be used in the arsenal of international counternuclear terrorism measures.

The principle of *aut dedere aut punire* ("extradite or prosecute") needs to be applied to terrorists. And the customary excepting of political offenses as reason for extradition must be abolished for most acts of terrorism. In this connection, the Canadian standard for political crimes, set down by the Canadian Federal Court of Appeal in 1972, would be a suitable model.[28] By this standard, the elements of a political act are so narrowly defined that virtually all acts of terrorism are patently criminal.

Although such a standard would appear to impair the prospects of even those legitimate rights to self-determination and human rights, actors proclaiming such rights cannot be exempted from the prevailing norms of humanitarian law. At the moment, the ideological motives of the accused are given far too much weight by states acting upon extradition requests. While ideological motive should be considered as a mitigating factor in the imposition of punishment, it must not be regarded as the basis for automatic immunity.[29] This principle was given eloquent expression by the delegate of Jordan to the Sixth Committee debate on international terrorism:

> (Jordan) believed in the legitimacy and dignity of national resistance against alien domination and oppression and also believed that the ethical rules of national resistance should be strict and humane; in this way, it would be possible to distinguish the national struggle

and resistance from the spirit of hate and violence which was the motivating force in all colonial and oppressive enterprises. It was imperative, in the interests of all movements of national liberation, to draw up and abide by a humanitarian code of ethics dissociated from any form of indiscriminate violence against innocent civilians or third parties.[30]

To understand the consequences of overemphasizing political motives for refusing extradition in matters concerning terrorism, one need only consider the case of several U.S. black militants who hijacked a Delta DC-8 jet from Miami to Algiers in 1972. In 1975, a French court refused a U.S. request for their extradition because their admitted crime had been inspired by "political motives." In November 1978, the group received very light sentences, ranging from 2½ to 3 years, in a trial hailed by the defense as a "slap at American racism" and a "trial on American history." In short, the hijacking was judged a political crime because of what was characterized as "a pattern of institutionalized racism in the United States" involving "police brutality, job discrimination, school segregation, poverty and hunger."

An even more flagrant abuse of the political offense grounds for refusing extradition took place in the same month of the French hijacking trial. In this case, Yugoslavia refused to extradite four West Germans wanted by Bonn on charges including the abduction and murder of Hanns-Martin Schleyer, an important industrialist. Moreover, instead of prosecuting the alleged terrorists themselves, Yugoslavia declared the four persona non grata and allowed them to leave "to a country of their own choice." Speculation suggests that this country was Libya, Iraq, or South Yemen.[31]

Under international law, the Yugoslavian action is improper for at least two reasons: (1) the political offense exception for refusing extradition must be waived in matters involving homicide; and (2) pursuant to long-standing customary norms and the spirit of a number of recent conventions (the Tokyo Convention of 1963; the Hague Convention of 1971; the Montreal

Convention of 1973; the Convention to Prevent and Punish
Acts of Terrorism Taking the Form of Crimes Against Persons
and Related Extortion that are of International Significance of
1973; and the United Nations Convention on the Prevention
and Punishment of Crimes Against Internationally Protected
Persons, which was signed in 1973), the extradite-or-prosecute
formula applies.

Of course, the Yugoslavian action illustrates a basic fact
about the outlook for improved international legal steps regarding extradition of terrorists. This fact is simply that individual
states base their extradition judgments primarily on narrow
political grounds. It follows that strategies of counterterrorism
should focus upon means to convince states that their own
long-term interests can never be served by proterrorist extradition decisions. To fail to recognize these strategies is to commit
the fallacy of "legalism" in the search for counterterrorist
procedures.

This does not mean, however, that the search for a fair,
precise, and comprehensive set of guidelines concerning jurisdiction and extradition should be abandoned altogether. Quite
the contrary! The identification of such a set of guidelines
could assist states in harmonizing their own judgments of self-
interest with explicit norms of international law. A particularly
promising set of such guidelines has already been formulated by
the participants in the Conference on Terrorism and Political
Crimes, June 4-16, 1972, in their Final Document:[32]

1. Insofar as it has been established that terrorism is an international
crime, any such offender should be effectively prosecuted and punished or
extradited to a requesting state. This position embodies the maxim *aut
dedere aut iudicare.*

2. Extradition to a requesting state should be granted in the absence
of prosecution by the requested state unless an international criminal
court is created with jurisdiction over such matters, in which case the
accused should be surrendered to the court's jurisdiction.

3. All states should be vested with universal jurisdiction with respect
to crimes of terrorism.

4. Whenever a state other than the state in which the act of terrorism was committed seeks to prosecute a terrorist, a reasonable number of observers from interested states and international organizations should be allowed to see the evidence and attend all proceedings.

5. When extradition is contemplated the ideological motives of the accused should not be the sole basis for the granting of asylum or for denying the extradition request.

6. Whenever an act of terrorism as defined herein is committed, or whenever other international crimes, i.e. crimes against humanity, grave breaches of the Geneva Conventions, or serious violation of fundamental human rights are committed, extradition should be granted regardless of the ideological motives of the actor.

7. In all other cases in which the political offense exception shall apply, the judge or other person making the decision must, *inter alia,* weigh the harm committed against the values sought to be preserved by the actor and the means employed in relationship to the goal pursued in light of the proportionality theory.

8. In the event of multiple extradition requests for the same offender, priority should be given to the requesting state relying on territorial jurisdiction in its request, followed by the state relying on the theory of protecting fundamental national interests.

9. The rights of the individual in extradition proceedings must always be upheld and he or she should not be precluded from raising any defenses available under extradition law and other relevant aspects of national and international law.

10. Extradition should not be granted when the individual sought is to be tried in an exceptional tribunal or under a procedure patently violative of fundamental human rights. In such cases, however, the requested state must prosecute the accused.

11. To avoid that requesting states resort to means other than extradition to secure a person, extradition procedures should be expedited but without sacrificing the protections afforded to the individuals. Furthermore, to ensure against unlawful seizure of persons, requested states who do not wish to extradite such an offender must prosecute them without unnecessary delay.

12. In order to ensure adequate administration of justice, judges, public officials and lawyers should be familiar with international criminal law and comparative law and those public officials directly involved should be specialists in the subject matter. Furthermore, it is recommended that special educational programs be established in legal institutions and other institutions of learning in the subject of international criminal law.

States must creatively interpret the Definition of Aggression approved by the General Assembly in 1974. This definition condemns the use of "armed bands, groups, irregulars or mercenaries, which carry out acts of armed force against another State," but supports wars of national liberation against "colonial and racist regimes or other forms of alien domination." Where it is interpreted too broadly, such a distinction leaves international law with too little leverage in counternuclear terrorist strategies. But where it is interpreted too narrowly, it places international law in the position of defending the status quo at all costs.

The problem, of course, is allowing international law to serve the interests of international order without impairing the legitimate objectives of international justice. But who is to determine the proper balance? Like all things human, force wears the Janus face of good and evil at the same time. It is an age-old problem, and one not adequately answered by identifying the institutional responsibility of the Security Council. The deliberate vagueness of the language of the Definition of Aggression is less of an obstacle than an opportunity if states can see their way clear to sensible ad hoc judgments.

But how can they make such judgments? What criteria can be applied to distinguish between legitimate claims for human rights and/or national liberation, and illegitimate acts of terror? Given the context of a decentralized system of international law, individual states must bear the ultimate responsibility for distinguishing between terrorists and "freedom fighters." What principles should inform their judgments?

Clearly, it is inadequate to suggest, as do the contributors to the Final Document of the Conference on Terrorism and Political Crimes, that "The resort to violence by individuals or groups engaging in wars of national liberation is lawful whenever it remains within the confines of international law which recognize such activities."[33] Such a suggestion is irremediably valueless since the pertinent "confines of international law which recognize such activities" have never been unambiguously stipulated. Nor does the idea of the just war, *jus ad bellum,* advance our interests, since that concept can be invoked on behalf of any position.[34]

At the moment, the only hope for appropriate criteria seems to lie in a deep and abiding concern for *discrimination* and *proportionality* in the use of force.[35] Once force begins to be applied to any segment of human population, blurring the distinction between combatants and noncombatants, terrorism has surfaced. Similarly, once force is applied to the fullest possible extent, constrained only by the limits of available weaponry, terrorism is taking place. In the words of the Report of the General Assembly's Ad Hoc Committee on International Terrorism in 1973: "Even when the use of force is legally and morally justified, there are some means, as in every form of human conflict, which must not be used; the legitimacy of a cause does not in itself legitimize the use of certain forms of violence, especially against the innocent." By itself, suffering cannot justify indiscriminacy and disproportionality in the use of force. As Elie Wiesel has argued, "Suffering confers neither privileges nor rights; it all depends on how one uses it. If you use it to increase the anguish of others, you are degrading, even betraying it."[36]

Perhaps the quintessence of the argument against suffering as justification for indiscriminacy and disproportionality is made by Elie Wiesel in the conclusion of his "Letter to a Young Palestinian Arab":

> I do feel responsible for what happened to you, but not for what you chose to do as a result of what happened to you. I feel responsible for your sorrow, but not for the way you use it, for in its name you have massacred innocent people, slaughtered children. From Munich to Maalot, from Lod to Entebbe, from highjacking to highjacking, from ambush to ambush, you have spread terror among unarmed civilians and thrown into mourning families already too often visited by death. You will tell me that all these acts have been the work of your extremist comrades, not yours; but they acted on your behalf, with your approval, since you did not raise your voice to reason with them. You will tell me that it is your tragedy which incited them to murder. By murdering, they debased that tragedy, they betrayed it. Suffering is often unjust, but it never justifies murder.[37]

6

Redefining National Interests: Planetization and Freedom from Nuclear Terrorism

In the final analysis, the effectiveness of international strategies of counternuclear terrorism will depend upon the tractability of proterrorist states. Real effectiveness, therefore, requires commitment by all states to unity and relatedness. To realize this commitment, all states will have to work toward the replacement of our fragile system of *realpolitik* with a new world politics of globalism.

Preventing nuclear terrorism must thus be seen as one part of an even larger strategy, one that is geared to the prevention of all forms of international violence.[1] It would be futile to try to tinker with the prospect of nuclear terrorism without affecting the basic structure of modern world politics. This structure is integral to all possibilities of an atomic apocalypse, and its re-visioning and reformation is central to all possibilities for survival.

The capacity to prevent nuclear terrorism is inseparable from a new consciousness by our national leaders. Amidst the precarious crosscurrents of global power relations, states must undertake prodigious efforts to resist the lure of primacy, focussing instead on the emergence of a new sense of global obligation. And these efforts must be undertaken very soon. The great French Enlightenment philosopher, Jean Jacques Rousseau, once remarked: "The majority of nations, as well as of men, are tractable only in their youth; they become incorrigible as they grow old." Understood in terms of the imperative to change direction in the search for peace, this suggests that unless these nations achieve such a change before losing their "youth," the chances for later success may be lost forever.

What is required, then, is a nuclear regime that extends the principles of nuclear war avoidance to the problem of nuclear terrorism. The centerpiece of this universal regime must be the cosmopolitan understanding that all states, like all people, form one essential body and one true community. Such an understanding, that a latent oneness lies buried beneath the manifold divisions of our fractionated world, need not be based on the mythical attractions of universal brotherhood and mutual concern. Instead, it must be based on the idea that individual states, however much they may dislike each other, are tied together in the struggle for survival.

To illustrate this principle, consider the following analogy: The states in world politics coexist in much the same fashion as a group of herdsmen who share a common pasture and who feel it necessary to increase their respective herds as best they can. Even though these herdsmen have determined that it is in the best interests of enlarging personal profits to continue to increase their own herds, they are mistaken. They are mistaken because they have failed to consider the *combined effect* of their calculations. This effect, of course, is an overgrazed pasture that brings them all to economic ruination.

In world politics, national leaders continue to act as if the security of their respective states is based upon national military power. Like the herdsmen, the failure of these leaders to understand the combined effect of such reasoning leads to the very opposite of the condition which they seek. It is a familiar pattern. So familiar, in fact, that one might expect the patently obvious defects of political "realism" to be scrupulously avoided. But they are not.

Consider one more analogy: The states in world politics are prone to act in the fashion of an audience in a crowded movie theater after someone has yelled "fire." Confronted with a sudden emergency, each member of the audience calculates that the surest route to safety is a mad dash for the nearest exit, no matter what might happen to others who happen to get in the way. The combined effect of such calculations, of course, is apt to be catastrophic. At any rate, it is apt to be much more unfortunate than would have been the case if the people in the audience had sought safety through cooperation.

In the manner of the people in the movie audience, states continue to misunderstand that their only safe course is one in which the well-being and security of each is determined from the standpoint of what is best for the system as a whole. The path to security that is founded upon the presumed advantages of preeminence in armaments is destined to fail. *Si vis pacem, para pacem.* If you want peace, prepare for peace. In order to avert the overwhelmingly destructive global nuclear catastrophe that is rooted in the "realist" path, decisive steps must be taken to involve world leaders in a more promising definition of national interest.

The time has come for states to struggle with the painful movements of a lungfish, forcing old fins to become new legs. For those that lock their definitions of national interest into the dying forms of realpolitik, there can be only disaster. Faced with the awareness that the wave length of change is now shorter than the life span of man, states must replace the intransigence of nationalisms with faith in a new kind of power. This is the primordial power of unity and interdependence, an ecumenical power that can replace the centrifugal forces that have atomized nations with a fresh vision of *realism*.

To achieve this faith, states must be surrounded by a new field of consciousness—one that flows from a common concern for the human species and from the undimmed communion of individual nations with the entire system of nations. Living at an interface between world order and global disintegration, states must slough off the shackles of outmoded forms of self-interest. With the explosion of the myth of "realism," the global society of states could begin to come together in a renewed understanding of the connection between survival and relatedness. When this happens, states will finally consummate their search for planetization.

The task, then, is to make the separate states conscious of their emerging planetary identity. With such a re-visioning of national goals and incentives, states can progress to an awareness of new archetypes for global society. Since all things contain their own contradiction, the world system based upon militaristic nationalism can be transformed into an organic world society.

To succeed in this task will be very difficult. But it need not be as fanciful as some would have us believe. Indeed, before we take the shroud measurements of the corpse of human society, we must understand that faith in the new forms of international interaction is a critical step toward their implementation.

Already, there is evidence that such faith is justified. We are, as philosopher William Irwin Thompson suggests, at the "edge of history." It is a time to reaffirm that the truest forms of realism lie in the imaginings of idealists. In the words of Thompson:

> In the history of ideas a new idea is often first picked up by a crazy person, then elaborated by an artist who is more interested in its imaginative possibilities than in its literal truth; then it is picked up by a scholar or scientist who has become familiar with the idea through the work of the artist; the savant makes the hitherto crazy idea perfectly acceptable to the multitude, until finally the idea rests as a certainty in the hands of a bureaucracy of pedants.[2]

Thompson's use of the term "crazy person" is, of course, laced with irony. In a world wherein "sane" foreign policy is still tied to the preposterous lies of a "peace through strength" ideology, "sanity" can lead only to oblivion. In such a world, only a "crazy person" can harbor the kind of consciousness that is needed for survival. Time, as St. Augustine wrote, is more than the present as we experience it and the past as a present memory. It is also the future as a present expectation, and this expectation carries within itself the seeds of its own verification.

To fulfill the expectations of a new global society, one based on a more advanced stage of world evolutionary development, appropriate initiatives must be taken *within* states. Here is the primary arena of world order reform. National leaders can never be expected to initiate the essential changes on their own. Rather, the new evolutionary vanguard must grow out of informed publics throughout the world. Such a vanguard, aiming to end the separation and competition of states that are founded upon egoistic definitions of national interest, has been described by Dr. Jonas Salk:

> A new body of conscious individuals exists, expressing its desire for a better life for Man as a species and as individuals, eager to devote themselves to this end. Such groups, when they are able to coalesce through an understanding of their relatedness to one another and to the natural processes involved in 'Nature's game' of survival and evolution, will find a strength and courage in sensing themselves as part of the Cosmos and as being involved in a game that is in accord with Nature and not anti-natural. These groups will initiate movements which, in turn, will be manifest in their effects not only upon the species and the planet but upon individual lives. Their benefit is likely to be expressed in a greater frequency, or proportion, of individuals finding increasing satisfaction and fulfillment in life.[3]

The vanguard that can change the destiny of the human race would act on the central understanding of Freud's great work, *Civilization and its Discontents.* Just as any civilization requires a renunciation of certain private instincts, so does an organic world society require a renunciation of certain "instincts" of states. Just as civilized man has exchanged a portion of his possibilities of happiness for security, so must nations exchange a portion of their "egoistic" preferences for a chance at survival. Like individual peoples of the distant past, modern states must learn to understand that their primal period of "everyone for himself" cannot endure for very long.

Freud tells us that the replacement of the power of the individual person by the power of the entire community constitutes the decisive act of civilization. Building upon this insight, we may say that the replacement of the power of the individual state by the power of the entire global community constitutes the decisive step of *planetization*. This power of the entire global community is not coercive military power, but the power of a universalized and new consciousness, a clear vision of reality that substitutes wholeness and convergence for the fatal instincts of "narcissism." In a struggle that Freud describes as a conflict between Eros and Death, between the instinct of life and the instinct of destruction, states must enter into the service of Eros, satisfying their vital needs in a spirit that recognizes the inter-relatedness of their fates.

If all of this sounds grandly unpolitical, it is because politics as usual cannot prevent nuclear terrorism. And if it all sounds hopelessly idealistic, it must be realized that nothing can be more fanciful than continuing on the present course. To be sure, today's idealists in foreign affairs—those who would seek to leave militaristically nationalistic states behind, whimpering in the corners of their egos—have little cause for optimism. Their search to actualize new forms of international interaction is unlikely to succeed. But it is the only search with even a re-mote chance of success; the only search worth conducting. It is, therefore, the only approach worthy of the term "realism."

But how, exactly, are we to begin this search? What can actually be done to bring about new forms of world politics? How can states reroute their narrowly self-interested mode of foreign policy activity to a more promising global orientation? How can national leaders begin to build upon the understand-ing that it is in their country's own best interests to develop strategies of international interaction from a systemic vantage point?

The answer, perhaps, lies in a self-conscious attempt to create an alternative configuration of world politics with which every state can identify the support of its own major preferences. As anyone can well imagine, this is no mean task. Indeed, there is an almost irresistible temptation to say with Schopenhauer, Spengler, and Tolstoy that any such attempt at global restructuring is the height of presumptuous nonsense. Can even the most gifted segments of humanity introduce an internationally selected and orderly movement into the *pluriversum* of modern world politics?

Clearly, in view of the heterogeneity of national value systems at work, this kind of configuration cannot reasonably expect to measure up to each state's optimal design, but it can still be *acceptable* to all of them. Scholars and statesmen can begin an expansive exploration of alternative world futures in an attempt to identify an appropriate "mix." Such exploration would be essential since planetization must rest upon a broad variety of compromises between states.

Dimensions for the Design of Alternative World Futures

There are three principal dimensions that might be used to characterize and "design" an improved system of world order. These dimensions are *Structure, Process,* and *Context.* By exploring a variety of global alternatives along each of these dimensions, statesmen and scholars can begin the urgently needed program of national and planetary restructuring that is a sine qua non for freedom from nuclear terrorism.

Structure

A number of ways exist of casting models of world order in terms of *structure,* i.e., the prevailing distribution of global power. Typically, these ways center on the distinction between bipolar and multipolar world systems.[4] There are, however, a number of more complex structural conceptualizations that might be considered. In exploring the planetization implications of such pattern-images, national decision makers and scholars may systematically address themselves to planetary design according to *structure.*

In fact, of course, this has already been done in the United States, first with the development of a Nixon-Ford-Kissinger foreign-policy doctrine favoring a pentagonal constellation of

world powers and now with a Carter agenda for continuing
global cooperation with allies, with the Soviet Union, and with
the People's Republic of China. There are, however, a great many
reasons to question the suitability of such a multipolar constellation. One of the most basic of these reasons concerns the alleged
connection between obstructing hegemonic tendencies and the
probability of peace. Even though the "new" balance system is
geared toward peace as its primary objective, and not toward
the prevention of hegemony per se, there is still no reason to
believe that the prevention of hegemony is actually productive
of peace.

There is no historical evidence that tends to support this doctrine's basic contention that the only time in the history of the
world that we have had any extended periods of peace is when
there has been a balance of power.[5] And there is no persuasive
logical argument that points to the general conclusion that it
is when one nation becomes more powerful in relation to its
potential competitor that the danger of war arises.[6] Indeed,
the first of these statements is entirely inaccurate while the
second ignores some of the most serious dangers that inhere in
today's nuclear system. From the standpoint of history, periods
of balance have inevitably yielded periods of war. From the
standpoint of logic, perceptions of balance in power relations
need have no effect on the likelihood of warfare, whatever its
form and whatever the nature of its participants.[7]

There is also no reason to believe that the "new" balance system is even capable of thwarting hegemony. In the first place,
there is an apparent contradiction between this objective and
the continuing U.S. commitment to "strength." While this commitment need not require actual U.S. domination of other
present and prospective powers, it very definitely presupposes
a condition of asymmetrical balance, a relationship of primus
inter pares.

In the second place, there is no reason to believe that even a
truly "symmetrical" balance (which neither the United States
nor the Soviet Union would ever encourage) would prevent

hegemony. This is the case because the prevailing doctrine necessarily rests upon the erroneous assumption that all of the major powers share a *preeminent* concern for preventing disproportionalities of power that lead to dominance, and that each major actor will act accordingly. The assumption that states always rank the prevention of hegemony at the apex of their particular preference orderings is erroneous because it suggests that such prevention is always believed by each state to be in its own best interests. In fact, there is certainly *no* reason to believe that states will consistently value the avoidance of hegemony more highly than alternative preferences. Any of the leading state actors in a symmetrical multipower balance system may, on occasion, calculate that the benefits that are expected to accrue from hegemony by any one state are great enough to warrant the probable costs.

But there is really no reason to dwell on the antihegemony implications of a symmetrical balance situation since such a situation is remarkably implausible. The principal members of the favored balance arrangement are patently asymmetrical. The United States and the Soviet Union are not well matched along the economic dimension, while Japan and Western Europe are military peers of neither superpower. And China's developing military power is still unparalleled on the economic front. It follows that a realistic analysis of the multipolar system must take as its starting point the idea of an asymmetrical balance— an idea that might very well be a glaring contradiction in terms.

A third reason for doubting that current multipolarism will be capable of preventing hegemony centers on the absence of a "swing" state or "balancer." Ironically, this feature of the new balance system touted as "proof" of departure from classical balance dynamics is actually a drawback from the standpoint of thwarting heady ideas by major powers. This is because a major power strongly committed to the balancer role and perceived as such by every other major power might magnify the anticipated costs of hegemony to the point where they would exceed prospective gains. Assuming that national decision makers choose rationally between alternative courses of action, this means that perceptions of a powerful and committed balancer might signal a crucial or even necessary input into the decisional calculi of states contemplating hegemony.

The multipolar balance system also contains an inherent contradiction between its commitment to more durable and strengthened alliances and its encouragement of multipolar tendencies. In effect, these are competing values. Alliance reliability is apt to be greater in bipolar world systems than in multipolar ones. The trend back toward the flexible alignments of the classical balance system that is signaled by the loosening of hierarchic ties within a major coalition represents a trend back toward mercurial forms of collaboration. This is because the reliability of alliances is apt to vary inversely with the number of system-wide axes of conflict.

The worthiness of multipolarism is also undercut by its essential reliance upon diplomacy and by its increased measure of decisional uncertainty. As a result of the expanded number of major actors and probable axes of conflict, would-be aggressor states would find it increasingly difficult to anticipate the retaliatory consequences of their actions. Such difficulty concerns the probable source as well as the substance of reciprocity. Although this increased measure of uncertainty might inhibit the willingness to aggress in certain instances, it very likely provides a less effective deterrent than that offered by the high probability of punishment associated with bipolar systems.

The increased uncertainty that characterizes multipolar world systems also creates specific disadvantages for counterterrorism. These disadvantages may manifest themselves via the activity of terrorist actors, or through the activities of their "host" states. In the first case, terrorists are able to parlay this uncertainty into greater freedom of action for themselves. This is because prospective state targets of terrorist actors would be apt to find it more difficult to rely upon alliance partners for support of antiterrorist measures in a multipolar world system. In the second case, "host" states whose foreign policies and power relations are affected by their terrorist "guests" may take aggressive steps toward other states more readily than they would in the less uncertain bipolar world.

This discussion points to the conclusion that the essential logic of peaceful global relations in a decentralized world system is thoroughly subverted by the operational dynamics of multipolarism. What all of this suggests, of course, is not the need to abandon multipolar conceptions in the search for an improved structural model of world order (at a minimum, the requirements of feasibility compel leaders and scholars to continue the search within a basic framework of multipolarism), but rather the need to improve the methodological underpinnings of this search. The adequacy of any structural alternative to the present system of world order is necessarily contingent upon the quality of the scholarship that leads to its formulation. In addressing themselves to planetary design according to structure, leaders and scholars must subject their tentative preferences to the scrutiny of sound logical analysis. Only then can they be in a position to determine gaps between alleged virtues and actual promise.

In order to narrow the gap between model and "reality," students of counternuclear terrorism needn't abandon their basic conceptualizations altogether. All they must do is subdivide those conceptualizations with the introduction of an important *intervening variable:* the power of terrorist actors. As an example, the scholar who wishes to preserve a bipolar characterization of world politics can simply create a variety of appropriate subcategories based upon terrorist power.

The actual number of these categories will depend upon the precise manner in which the intervening variable is described (e.g., if it is treated dichotomously—large extent, small extent—there will be two subcategories; if it is treated trichotomously—large extent, moderate extent, small extent—there will be three subcategories, etc.). Of course, this manner of subdivision may be applied to multipolar, multibloc, or any other basic structural models as well. In this way, scholars may reconcile their principal characterizations of structure with the increasing influence of terrorist actors.

The most basic way in which terrorist power may be introduced into existing structural models is simply to note whether or not such power exists at all. This means introducing a dichotomous distinction between terrorist actors sharing in the power and such actors not sharing in the power. Where the underlying world system structure is described as bipolar, a ready-made set of models becomes available. Figure 1 describes the conceptions of Wolfram Hanrieder:[8]

Professor Hanrieder subdivides the bipolar universe of cases according to (1) the ratio of power between blocs, and (2) whether or not secondary actors share in the power. The two kinds of bipolarity treated (symmetrical—equal ratio of power between blocs; asymmetrical—unequal ratio of power between blocs) become "hetero" systems whenever secondary actors enter into the picture. These secondary actors, however, refer to *states.* Nowhere do they extend to terrorist actors.

But this does not prevent us from "translating" the Hanrieder models to suit our own purposes. Indeed, where we tie our definition of secondary actors to terrorist actors, these models provide exactly what is needed. Here, "hetero" systems become those forms of bipolarity in which certain distinct kinds of *nonstate actors* share in the power.

These models immediately reveal an important pattern of

Figure 1.
Models of Bipolar World System Structure

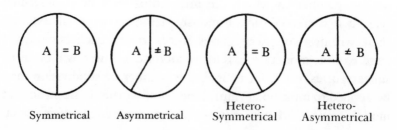

Symmetrical   Asymmetrical   Hetero-   Hetero-
                                       Symmetrical   Asymmetrical

interdependence in bipolar systems. This pattern concerns the relationship between the ratio of power between blocs and the extent of terrorist power. Not only does the ratio of power between blocs seriously affect the extent of terrorist power, but this extent in turn affects the ratio of power between blocs.

This kind of ongoing interaction may have serious implications for the student of counternuclear terrorism. The point of the *redefined* heterosymmetrical and heteroasymmetrical models is twofold: (1) they may *alert* the scholar to the relationship in the first place; or (2) they may allow for accurate conceptualization once the relationship has been detected in some other manner, i.e., after a number of historical materials have been scrutinized. Just which purpose the models will serve in any given case depends upon the individual scholar's particular strategy of inquiry (whether he prefers to begin by scrutinizing abstract models or empirical cases).

One way in which terrorist actors may affect ths ratio of power between blocs is by exerting influence on their "host" states.

Terrorist actors may have a particularly important effect on their host states' collective defense arrangements. Depending upon the relationship between these actors and their state hosts, the alliance position of the latter may vary considerably. More exactly, where this is the kind of relationship in which the host state is in full control of terrorist activities, there exists no special reason to doubt the credibility of its alliance commitments. On the other hand, where the state actor is clearly an unwilling host and not in complete control of terrorist activities, its prospective ability to honor alliance commitments may be seriously undermined. The cumulative effects of this kind of relationship between host states and terrorist actors may, in turn, seriously affect the ratio of power between blocs.

In exploring the ways in which terrorist actors influence the ratio of power between blocs, we may also assess their affects on alliances generally. For one thing, the pressure of terrorist actors may affect the *number* of alignments between states.

It may occasion additional alliances among states that are commonly opposed to terrorist activities, inhibit prospective alliances where split sympathies are in evidence, or even break up existing alignments that are crosscut by this kind of split. In certain instances, this sort of breakup might result in new and different alignments and perhaps even an entirely new global structure. If the original structure were a "tight" bipolar one, it might be transmuted into some form of "loose" bipolarity. If it were "loose" bipolar to begin with, it might be transformed into a multipolar system.

The ratio of power between blocs may also affect the extent of terrorist power. Just *how* it affects this depends largely on (1) whether the blocs are split in their sympathies to terrorist actors, and (2) the extent to which the ratio of power between blocs is paralleled by this split. For example, if the blocs were split in their feelings about terrorist actors along bloc lines and the more powerful bloc were sympathetic, these actors could expect a far more satisfactory context for their efforts than they would if the situation were reversed. There operating milieu would be less propitious were the more powerful bloc the unsympathetic one. In those cases where feelings toward terrorist actors are *not* divided along bloc lines, there is no reason to believe that the ratio of power between blocs is particularly important to terrorist power.

More complex conceptualizations of multipolarity. To this point, we have considered ways in which terrorist power may be introduced into *bipolar* models as an intervening variable. More exactly, we have shown that the Hanrieder models can be redefined such that "hetero" systems become those forms of bipolarity in which terrorist actors (rather than state actors) share in the power. While no ready-made models exist for multipolar world systems in this sense, there is no reason to believe that they are intrinsically less susceptible to subdivision.

Scholars who wish to characterize the basic system structure as *multipolar* while taking terrorist actors into account may begin with the simple distinction between (1) multipolar power systems in which terrorist actors do not share in the power and (2) multipolar power systems in which terrorist actors do share in the power. Thereafter, the second class of cases may be subdivided according to the prevailing ratio of power between *national actors* (rather than blocs, as in the bipolar case). This ratio may have important implications for terrorist power. Alternatively, terrorist power may have decisive consequences for the ratio of power between national actors.

For example, terrorist power may affect the ratio of power between national actors in much the same way as it affects the ratio of power between blocs in a bipolar system. These means include the exertion of pressure on host states and the instigation or breakup of various kinds of interstate alignments.

Terrorist power may also affect the ratio of power between national actors in other ways. One way concerns the formation of "heterogeneous" alignments, i.e., alignments between state and terrorist actors. Such collaboration may strengthen the state partners by offering them a means of acting "through" their nonstate allies. As we know, this new opportunity for acting with impunity may greatly increase the likelihood of international aggression.

Another way in which terrorist power may affect the ratio of power between national actors concerns the formation of alliances in which both parties are terrorist actors. To an increasing extent, terrorist organizations are claiming *de jure* status for themselves, negotiating agreements with each other in the process. The cumulative effects of these counterstate alignments may be profoundly important. In the most obvious sense, they may contribute to the overthrow of established governments or established policies. The ratio of power between national actors may also affect the extent of terrorist power in multipolar systems. As in the case of bipolar systems, where the appropriate ratio is between *blocs,* the importance of the ratio of power between national actors depends largely on the prevailing pattern of sympathies toward terrorist actors and on the extent to which this pattern is paralleled by differences in power.

Where national actors are split in their feelings toward terrorist actors, the power of the latter will depend to a significant extent upon the ratio of power between the sympathetic and unsympathetic states. Terrorist power will be enhanced to the extent that sympathetic states are more powerful, and diminished to the extent that unsympathetic states have the upper hand. If, however, the power of sympathetic and unsympathetic states were roughly equal, the ratio of power between national actors would be unimportant to terrorist power. Similarly, if national actors were *not* split in their feelings toward terrorist actors, the ratio of power between the former would be of no particular importance to terrorist power. Such a condition might exist if virtually all state actors were of one opinion on this question, irrespective of what that particular opinion might be.

This information about the bases of terrorist power can now be used to create more useful structural conceptualizations of the world system. To this point, our discussion of both bipolar and multipolar systems has simply centered upon terrorist actors sharing in the power. No formal use has yet been made of the particular extent of sharing involved. Using the information from the above discussion, however, both bipolar and multipolar systems in which terrorist actors share in the power may now be subdivided further according to the degree of sharing in evidence.

Bipolarity. Our earlier discussion of bipolarity centered on two basic models. Each of these models was characterized by the presence of terrorist actors. The difference between them concerned the ratio of power between blocs. This ratio was equal in the heterosymmetrical system and unequal in the heteroasymmetrical one.

With the introduction of the extent of terrorist power as an intervening variable, each of these basic universes of cases may be broken down further. Exactly how many subcases may be created from the heterosymmetrical and heteroasymmetrical systems will depend upon the way the intervening variable is treated. If it is treated dichotomously (e.g., large extent, small extent), there will be four basic patterns rather than two:

Heterosymmetrical	Heteroasymmetrical
a. large extent	a. large extent
b. small extent	b. small extent

If it is treated trichotomously (e.g., large extent, moderate extent, small extent), there will be six basic patterns, and so on. The advantage of this kind of subdivision is that it facilitates accurate structural modeling of world politics. At the same time, care must be taken to avoid the construction of too many "boxes." Any model is necessarily a simplification, and while accurate representation is a primary objective, it must not be accomplished at the expense of generality. It follows that anything more complex than trichotomous treatment of our intervening variable is likely to yield a too-large number of structural models.

Multipolarity. In our discussion of multipolarity, we had no ready-made set of models at hand. Unlike the bipolar case, therefore, we spoke of no particular number of basic configurations. Rather, we implied that there could be as many multipolar models with terrorist actors under investigation as there were ways of characterizing the ratio of power between national actors. If this intervening variable were treated dichotomously (e.g., equal, unequal) there would be two basic models. If equality and inequality might coexist at different levels of the system (e.g., the presence of a major power–minor power distinction signifies a condition of inequality between classes of actors that might be paralleled by equality within one or both classes), a trichotomous treatment of the intervening variable would become possible. Here, we would speak of an equal ratio, an unequal ratio, and a "mixed" or equal-unequal ratio. In this case there would be three basic models of multipolar world systems.

With the extent of terrorist power as a second intervening variable, each of these basic multipolar models or universes of cases may be subdivided further. Once again, exactly how many additional cases may be created depends upon the particular manner in which the extent of terrorist power is handled. If we start with the two basic multipolar systems mentioned above, and treat the second intervening variable dichotomously, we will have four new universes of cases:

Equal Ratio	Unequal Ratio
a. large extent	a. large extent
b. small extent	b. small extent

If we start with the two basic multipolar systems, and treat extent of terrorist power trichotomously, we will construct six new universes of cases:

Equal Ratio	Unequal Ratio
a. large extent	a. large extent
b. moderate extent	b. moderate extent
c. small extent	c. small extent

If we start out with the three basic multipolar systems mentioned, and treat the second intervening variable dichotomously, we will also have six new universes of cases. But these, of course, will be somewhat different from the earlier set of six (two will be new, while two that were present in the first set of six will be absent in the second):

Equal Ratio	Mixed Ratio	Unequal Ratio
a. large extent	a. large extent	a. large extent
b. small extent	b. small extent	b. small extent

Finally, if we start with the three basic multipolar systems and treat the extent of terrorist power trichotomously as well, we will create nine new universes of cases:

Equal Ratio	Mixed Ratio	Unequal Ratio
a. large extent	a. large extent	a. large extent
b. moderate extent	b. moderate extent	b. moderate extent
c. small extent	c. small extent	c. small extent

What have been created here are several new structural models of world politics. By taking into account the power of terrorist actors as well as of states, these models provide much more accurate renderings of global structure than their more basic "parent" ones. At the same time, they are not yet "too complex." Their creation is informed by the introduction of a limited number of intervening variables into the basic bipolar and multipolar models. Any one of these new models may now be investigated from the standpoint of planetization and freedom from nuclear terrorism.

Hypotheses and Models. These models must not be investigated at random. The choice of models for investigation must be determined by a particular problem in question and by suggested explanations for that problem. In short, inquiry must begin with specific hypotheses and models must be selected accordingly. The models provide the context within which hypotheses may be explored. To investigate the models without the benefit of particular hypotheses is to put the cart before the horse. In such cases, there exists no criterion by which to determine what facts are relevant to the exploration of the model. Here, "explanation" is backward.

For example, if we were interested in discovering the effects of terrorist presence on power management (war avoidance) in bipolar systems, we might advance an appropriate hypothesis. To begin to explore the hypothesis we would create two basic bipolar models, one without the presence of terrorist actors and the other with such presence. Now, suppose that we were also interested in the ratio of power between blocs in these systems. More exactly, suppose that we were to hypothesize that in bipolar systems with terrorist actors, power management is more effective if the ratio between blocs is equal than if it is unequal. To evaluate this hypothesis, we would turn to the redefined heterosymmetrical and heteroasymmetrical models described earlier.

Similarly, if we were interested in discovering the effects of terrorist presence on power management in multipolar systems, we might advance the following hypothesis: the effectiveness of power management in multipolar systems decreases as terrorist actors enter the scene. To begin to explore this hypothesis we would examine two forms of multipolarity, one without terrorist actors and the other with such actors. And if we were to hypothesize further that where terrorist actors are present, power management is more effective if the ratio of power between national actors is equal than if it is unequal, the second multipolar model would be subdivided. Of the resultant two models, one would have an equal ratio of power and the other an unequal ratio.

If we were interested in the relative effects of terrorist actors on power management in bipolar and multipolar systems, we would hypothesize a particular relationship comparing these effects. To investigate this hypothesis, it would be necessary to explore at least two basic models: a bipolar one and a multipolar one, each with the presence of terrorist actors. If we were to modify the hypothesis by introducing ratio of power (between blocs or national actors) as an intervening variable, we would explore at least four basic models. This is because each original model would be subdivided according to whether the ratio were equal or unequal. If ratio of power were treated trichotomously, we would explore six basic models. Here, each original model would be subdivided according to whether the ratio were equal, mixed, or unequal.

We might also be concerned with *extent* of terrorist power in various systems. For example, if we were interested in the connection between such extent and power management, we might explore various subsets of the basic bipolar or multipolar models. These models would differ from each other according to the extent of terrorist power. If this intervening variable is treated dichotomously (large extent, small extent) we are left to explore four structural models. If it is treated trichotomously (large extent, moderate extent, small extent), we are left to treat six new models.

The number of models we must consider increases even more if we extend our concern to the ratio of power factor mentioned earlier. This means that where we are interested in the connection between extent of terrorist power and power management and in the ratio of power between blocs or national actors, the basic models must first be broken down along the ratio dimension. If this dimension is treated dichotomously, each basic model would be described as equal or unequal. If it is treated trichotomously, each basic model would be equal, mixed, unequal. However it is treated, the resultant models would then be broken down, as before, according to the extent of terrorist power. Where this extent is treated as large, moderate, or small, this may mean the exploration of as many as six models for the bipolar case and nine for the multipolar one. These models might also be used for comparisons between bipolar and multipolar world systems.

Finally, if we were interested in the transmutation of decentralized global politics into a system of collective security, we might hypothesize a particular relationship between structure and collective security success. For example, it might be hypothesized that bipolar world systems are more favorable to the success of collective security than multipolar ones. To explore this hypothesis would require the creation of the basic bipolar and multipolar models.

Let us actually begin to investigate the hypothesis and see where it leads us. This requires consideration of the basic bipolar and multipolar models. Once again, it suggests that bipolar world systems are more conducive to collective security success than multipolar ones.

Why should this be the case? A comparison of the two models indicates a smaller number of "peripheries" in the bipolar case. This implies a decline in uncertainty—a decline that makes it easier for any national actor to determine the reciprocal behavior of other national actors. For an actor to decide that compliance with collective-security dictates is a gainful course of action, it must believe that its own compliance will be paralleled by the compliance of a critical number of other actors.

The bipolar model is also characterized by two leading national actors with preeminent power positions. This fact tends to reduce the number of individual national decisions needed for general compliance with collective security requirements. Hence, so long as the leading actors themselves are partial to collective security, their preeminence makes collective security success more likely.

Now, within the bipolar class of cases, further distinctions can be made. For example, we might hypothesize that "tight" bipolarity is even more favorable to collective security success than "loose" bipolarity. To explore this hypothesis, we must create "tight" and "loose" bipolar models. These subsets of bipolarity differ from each other in that the latter form contains a number of national actors that exist apart from the membership of the two blocs.

Why should "tight" bipolarity be favored? A comparison of the two bipolar forms indicates that the shift from tight to loose conditions frees an increasing number of national actors to strive for security "privately" rather than collectively. Such a shift has the effect of increasing the effective number of independent national actors. This shift also means that national actors may move freely between poles in cementing alliances. This broadens the number of possible interaction opportunities between these actors. As a result, the power of the leading actors is diminished. So long as such power is judged helpful to collective security success, the shift from tight to loose bipolarity must be regretted. In this case it makes it more difficult for the leading actors to ensure the compliance of other national actors.

Finally, a distinction might even be introduced into the tight bipolar class of cases. This distinction concerns the ratio of power between blocs. It appears plausible to hypothesize that within the tight bipolar category, an equal ratio of power between blocs is preferable to an unequal ratio. This is because an inequality of power between poles may offer an incentive to the more powerful bloc to magnify the advantages of private rather than collective security. To explore this hypothesis, we would have to create two subsets of the tight bipolar universe, with the difference between them being the ratio of power between blocs.

We have advanced the case for new structural models of world politics. These models would take theoretical account of terrorist actors. They could be constructed without abandoning prevailing conceptualizations such as bipolarity or multipolarity, but simply by introducing terrorist actors into these conceptualizations. This has the effect of subdividing basic models into more complex ones.

With such models in hand, scholars might offer far more accurate representations of world politics. And they might use these representations to examine a variety of important hypotheses relating to the requirements of planetization. As in the cases already mentioned, these hypotheses might concern the power management or war avoidance features of global systems. Or they might concern other important dependent variables such as system transformation, stability, or national power. *Whatever* the subject to be explained, these new structural models would be apt to yield more productive insights into elements of counternuclear terrorism.

Not only would these models be useful for investigating certain extant hypotheses, but they might also suggest interesting hypotheses in the first place. While it is true that the selection of models for investigation must depend upon the particular hypothesis in question, and that—strictly speaking—models *follow* hypotheses, the models might raise additional new hypotheses for later inquiry. In the course of investigating a new structural model derived from the hypothesis of the moment, the analyst may become aware of new patterns and relationships that yield still more hypotheses and perhaps even more models. Hence, new structural models serve a dual role: they provide the context for exploring various hypotheses and they inspire the creation of new hypotheses. Both roles encourage the development of a more comprehensive and coherent system of counternuclear terrorist theory.

In view of the terrible urgency of nuclear terrorism, an improved system of theory represents the necessary first step to planetization. Without such a system of theory there can be no promising attempts to reorder the planet, no movement toward purposeful control of the search for new global forms.

Process

The second design dimension to be considered here concerns the processes of global power management. While there are an extraordinary variety of conceivable arrangements for managing global power, three basic types of arrangement come immediately to mind: balance of power, collective security, and world government. These types are defined in terms of the degree of centralization exhibited. Hence, the balance of power system is the least centralized, the world government system is the most centralized, and collective security falls in between the two polar forms.[9]

Typically, scholars have argued for the advantages of increasing centralization. Such arguments derive from the assumption that the actors in world politics cannot coexist peacefully without an authority above them. From Dante in the fourteenth century to Clark and Sohn, Falk, and Mendlovitz in the twentieth, the idea has held sway that world leaders must replace anarchy in world politics with the conditions of civil order.[10]

While it is by no means self-evident that the effectiveness of power management parallels increasing centralization, it is certain that world leaders seeking planetization would opt for a replacement for the existing balance of power arrangement. In this arrangement, states are confronted with the very condition that impels them to look for alternatives: a configuration of forces wherein states define their own interests in competitive terms and in which security is mistakenly identified with the improvement or preservation of relative power position. This configuration is bound to break down calamitously in the not-too-distant future.

This brings world leaders and scholars contemplating *process* design changes to collective security models of world order. Here, the ultimate right to make decisions concerning the use of international force is transferred from individual states to some specially established center of sovereign-authority, while the actual instruments of force remain exclusively at the level of individual states. It is a condition where the prerogative to use international force is unsupported by force.

How are world leaders and scholars likely to react to this kind of *process* alternative? Upon inspecting the collective security arrangement, its central problem becomes immediately apparent. Calculating that the benefits of compliance with collective security system directives are outweighed by the costs unless a condition of *general* compliance is anticipated, each state is apt to continue its reliance upon "private" methods of security seeking. After all, the absence of force in collective security repositories will raise grave doubts about the reciprocal compliance of every other state.

This does not mean, however, that collective security can never succeed. There are a variety of design changes that might seriously affect the decisional calculi of states, causing them to develop far greater confidence in the belief that their own prospective compliance with collective security directives would be generally paralleled.

What are these changes? They include a diminished number of actors, homogeneity as to type of actor and state government, "status-quo" rather than "revolutionary-modernizing" actors, and a "tight" condition of bipolarity in which the ratio of power between the two blocs is roughly equal. In principle, these alterations might contribute importantly to overcoming the central impediment to collective security success: the understanding of states that their own willingness to seek security cooperatively rather than competitively will not be widely enough imitated. In fact, however, such alterations would be very difficult to produce by leaders and scholars contemplating planetary redesign along collective security lines.

Finally, scholars and world leaders thinking about planetary redesign in *process* terms might settle upon one form or another of world government. To do so would be to place themselves squarely in the tradition of the most heavily favored orientation to world peace. It does not mean, however, that they would certainly be opting for the most effective form of global power management. Contrary to widely held opinion, a condition of world government is not self-evidently better than less-centralized configurations. The requirements of effective war prevention are extraordinarily complex, and each particular conception of world government must be examined on its own unique merits.

Whatever the peculiar nuances of a world government process, each instance of this class of cases is characterized by the same essential distribution of force and sovereign authority. That is, the ultimate right to make decisions concerning international force is the property of some specially established global center that is endowed with some measure of force. Unlike the collective security model, therefore, sovereign directives emanating from the central authority in a world government situation are supported by force.

How effective is power management in such a system? Is it necessarily more effective than in the collective security system, as is usually believed? Upon inspection, statesmen and scholars will quickly perceive an important difference between the two kinds of centralized arrangements for managing world power. This difference is that the central authority in the world government system possesses some force of its own, and that world government is thus apt to be a more propitious circumstance for undercutting the tragedy of the commons. As central force now exists to enforce compliance, each state is presumably less uncertain about the willingness of other states to comply. Hence, each state is more willing to regard compliance with the dictates of centralized management as a potentially gainful course of action.

Taken by itself, however, the existence of a central force repository is insufficient to ensure widespread compliance. National decision makers must also believe that these forces are generally held to be (1) sufficiently invulnerable to first-strike attack, and (2) capable of penetrating a would-be aggressor's active defenses. Where these traits are in doubt, the deterrent quality of centralized forces dissolves.

Moreover, however large, powerful, and invulnerable these centralized forces might appear, their controlling authorities must also be judged willing to use them. For states to believe in the deterrent effectiveness of a specially constituted central authority, and hence in that authority's ability to overcome the tragedy of the commons, they must perceive that that authority is not only widely recognized as capable of delivering an unacceptably damaging retaliatory strike, but that it is also generally believed willing to do so. Perceived willingness, then, is an essential ingredient of the world government center's deterrence posture.

From what we have just discussed, world leaders and scholars exploring the desirability of a world government approach to world security would be mistaken to assume that increasing global centralization is self-evidently worthwhile. Even where a specially constituted central authority possesses some force of its own, successful deterrence need not be assured. This is because such success requires the belief of states that the central authority is willing to carry out its threats of retaliation, and that its forces are sufficiently invulnerable to preemptive attacks or to subsequent attempts at active defense. These requirements are exceedingly complex. They must not be overlooked by prospective designers of an alternative world order.

Context

A final dimension to be considered by world leaders and scholars groping toward planetization concerns the prevailing weapons technology context of world politics. While there are a great many ways in which global patterns can be characterized along this particular dimension, the most obvious and important one centers on the conventional/nuclear distinction. In short, system-directed planetary designers might contemplate the most propitious kind of distribution of the instruments of two qualitatively distinct powers of destruction.

From what we already know, world leaders must take steps to curtail the proliferation of nuclear weapons. With such proliferation, the world system moves closer and closer to the true

Hobbesian state of nature—a condition of "dreadful equality" in which "the weakest has strength enough to kill the strongest." This condition, of course, has frighteningly destabilizing implications for global security. Consider the following five points concerning the requirements and limitations of nuclear deterrence:

1. The tremendous power of destruction that accompanies a nuclear weapons capability does not automatically bestow safety from aggression. The success of nuclear deterrence rests not only upon perceptions of explosive power, but also upon perceptions of willingness to use such power. Such willingness may not always be present. And even where it is present, instances might arise where prospective aggressors fail to recognize it. In these instances, nuclear deterrence could fail even though a nuclear-weapon state had actually committed itself to threat fulfillment. With the proliferation of nuclear weapons, this sort of failure would become increasingly likely.

2. The success of nuclear deterrence also requires secure nuclear retaliatory forces, i.e., forces that are not susceptible to nullification by a first-strike attack. The condition of secure nuclear forces, however, is not only difficult to satisfy, it is especially difficult in the case of prospective members of the "Nuclear Club." It follows that the prospect of preemptive or first-strike attacks would be intolerably high in a world with an expanding number of nuclear weapon states. Moreover, to protect against preemption, new nuclear powers would almost certainly adopt "hair trigger" strategies for weapons release that would heighten the hazards of accidental or inadvertent firings.

3. The greater the number of nuclear powers, the greater the probability of catastrophic nuclear accidents or accidental nuclear wars. This is the case not only because of the multiplication of present risks, but also because these risks are certain to be aggravated in a proliferated global context. New nuclear powers would be unlikely to adopt the sophisticated sorts of redundant safeguards against inadvertent firings that are now in use by the superpowers. New nuclear powers would also be apt to initiate imprecise command/control procedures that might

render the proper locus of authority difficult to determine.

4. The greater the number of nuclear powers, the greater the likelihood of nuclear weapons use by unauthorized personnel. New nuclear powers would be apt to use fewer, less sophisticated safeguards against unauthorized use than the superpowers. And they might also increase the number of decision makers who are authorized to use nuclear weapons.

5. The greater the number of nuclear powers, the greater the probability of nuclear weapons use by irrational national leaders. Should irrational leaders get hold of nuclear weapons, they might very well initiate nuclear strikes against other nuclear states even though enormously destructive or even annihilating retaliation were anticipated. Here, the so-called logic of nuclear deterrence would break down completely, and—perhaps—irretrievably.[11]

Understanding these points, leaders and scholars examining the context-design dimension must begin to identify strategies for halting the spread of nuclear weapons. As we have already seen, such strategies must concern not only the "horizontal" spread of nuclear weapons to states that are not yet members of the nuclear club, but also the "vertical" spread that is implied by the U.S.–USSR strategic arms race. Although some progress is now underway, a great deal still remains to be done.

Conclusion

We have now seen how an improved system of world order—a system of planetization that is essential to freedom from nuclear terrorism—might be conceptualized using three design dimensions. Of course, it is one thing to talk about the conceptualization of alternative global societies and another to take actual steps toward the implementation of such societies. Nevertheless, however infeasible it might appear, the creation of a new world order within which states can begin to maximize their preferences cooperatively rather than competitively is integral to avoiding nuclear terrorism. There is no other way. To stay within the present system of world order—the time-dishonored *bellum omnes contra omnes*—is certainly more feasible, but it is hardly more realistic since this system cannot last out the century.

What can be done to hasten the serious exploration of alternative world futures and—ultimately—to implement appropriate forms of system transformation? For a beginning, national leaders must begin to expand upon the principles articulated by President Carter in his speech at the University of Notre Dame:

> For too many years, we have been willing to adopt the flawed and erroneous principles and tactics of our adversaries, sometimes abandoning our own values for theirs. We have fought fire with fire, never thinking that fire is better quenched with water. This approach failed, with Vietnam the best example of its intellectual and moral poverty.[12]

To succeed in such expansion, world leaders must learn to understand and accept the inescapable interrelatedness of their national destinies.

At the moment, world leaders continue to act on the mistaken assumption that their long-standing foreign policies of "everyone for himself" can be conducted indefinitely without fatal consequences. To replace this sort of understanding with a new affirmation of global singularity and solidarity would represent a natural starting point for the essential restructuring of national and world political life. As far as effective strategies of counternuclear terrorism are concerned, there is no better starting point.

States, like individual persons, are cemented to each other not by haphazard aggregation, but by the certainty of their basic interdependence. Beneath the diversities of a seemingly fractionated world, there exists a basic oneness. With this manifestation of the "one in the many," states may begin to aim at particular goals and objectives in harmony with all other states. With an integral vision sparked by the impulse of global solidarity, states may begin to produce refinements in their relationship that can bring them back from the brink. Unlike anything else, this vision can endow the search for planetization and freedom from nuclear terrorism with real potency.

Notes

Chapter 1

1. See Joseph A. Camilleri, *Civilization in Crisis: Human Prospects in a Changing World* (Cambridge: Cambridge University Press, 1976), p. 11.

2. See *Report of the Ad Hoc Committee on International Terrorism,* United Nations, General Assembly, 1973, Official Records, 28th Session, Supplement No. 28, A/9028, p. 21.

3. Article 3 (g) states: "The sending by or on behalf of a State of armed bands, groups, irregulars or mercenaries, which carry out acts of armed force against another State of such gravity as to amount to the acts listed above, or its substantial involvement therein." Cited in Benjamin B. Ferencz, *Defining International Aggression: The Search for World Peace,* vol. 2 (New York: Oceana, 1975), p. 17.

4. On October 24, 1970, the General Assembly adopted the following Declaration on Principles of International Law Concerning Friendly Relations and Cooperation Among States:

> Every State has the duty to refrain from organizing, instigating, assisting or participating in acts of civil strife or terrorist acts in another State or acquiescing in organized activities within its territory directed towards the commission of such acts, when the acts referred to in the present paragraph involve a threat or use of force.
>
> However, this same Declaration includes even greater emphasis on the "principle of equal rights and self-determination of peoples."
>
> Every State has the duty to refrain from any forcible action which deprives people referred to above in the elaboration of the present principles of their right to self-determination and freedom and independence. In their actions against, and resistance to, such forcible action in pursuit of the exercise of their right to self-determination, such peoples are entitled to seek and to receive support in accordance with the purposes and principles of the Charter. (See *Yearbook of the United Nations 1970,* New York, UN, Office of Public Information, 1971, pp. 790-791.)

5. See Ferencz, *Defining International Aggression,* p. 18.

6. Cited by Walter Laqueur, ed., *The Terrorism Reader: A Historical Anthology from Aristotle to the IRA and the PLO* (New York: New American Library, 1978), p. 16.

7. See Sergey Nechaev, *Catechism of the Revolutionist,* 1869, cited in Laqueur, ed., *The Terrorism Reader,* p. 68.

8. See Curtis Bill Pepper, "The Possessed," *New York Times Magazine,* February 18, 1979, p. 32.

9. However, even those terrorist groups with distinctly identifiable political objectives must be distinguished from the "classical" revolutionary. The revolutionary seeks to "seize power," usually by a frontal assault on the centers of political control. Using such methods as the general strike and the occupation of military, police, and industrial bases, he/she avoids random actions against peripheral targets. Force is used, but almost never with deliberation against innocent parties.

10. See David Fromkin, "The Strategy of Terrorism," *Foreign Affairs,* vol. 53, no. 4, July 1975, p. 685.

11. See Hannah Arendt, *On Violence* (New York: Harcourt, Brace and World, 1970), p. 5.

12. A Central Intelligence Agency Research Study offers the following "elementary typology" of terrorist groups:

> Particularistic (ethnic, religious, linguistic, or regional); Nationalistic (irredentist or anti-colonial); Ideological, Anarchism, Radical Left (revolutionary socialists, Trotskyites, Maoists, Guevarists, Castroites, and other ultra-left fringe groups); Orthodox Communism, Extreme Right, Other; Pathological. (See *International and Transnational Terrorism: Diagnosis and Prognosis,* April 1976, p. 35.)

13. In this connection, it should be pointed out that Marx did not believe in individual terrorism and that both Lenin and Trotsky had serious reservations about indiscriminate terrorism. Contemporary Communist parties maintain a doctrinal opposition to most terror tactics and generally avoid such tactics in pursuit of their objectives. In fact, such groups as the Italian Red Brigades are largely a response to the "revisionism" of established Communist parties, and there is considerable irony in their association of terrorism with a "true Communism."

14. See U.S., Congress, House, Committee on Internal Security, *Terrorism,* 93rd Cong., August 1, 1974, pp. 71-73.

15. See Research Study, Central Intelligence Agency, *International and Transnational Terrorism,* pp. 16-17.

16. See Charles A. Russell and Bowman H. Miller, "Profile of a Terrorist," *Terrorism: An International Journal,* vol. 1, no. 1, 1977, pp. 17-34.

17. Ibid., p. 17.

Chapter 2

1. See, for example, CIA Research Study, *International and Transnational Terrorism: Diagnosis and Prognosis,* April 1976.

2. For detailed information concerning Department of Defense directives dealing with nuclear weapons custody and accountability procedures, and nuclear weapons physical and storage security, see: DOD Directive 5210.41, July 30, 1974, *Security Criteria and Standards for Protecting Nuclear Weapons*; DOD Directive 5210.42, April 24, 1975, *Nuclear Weapon Personnel Reliability Program*; DOD Directive 4540.3, December 19, 1972, *Logistic Movement of Nuclear Weapons*; DOD Instruction 4540.4, December 20, 1972, *Safety Standards and Procedures for the Logistic Movement of Nuclear Weapons*; DOD Directive 5030.15, August 8, 1974, *Safety Studies and Reviews of Nuclear Weapons Systems*; and DOD Directive 5100.1, December 31, 1958, revised 1969, *Functions of the Department of Defense and its Major Components.*

3. See Bob Wiedrich, "Nuclear Weapons Ripe for Plucking," *Chicago Tribune,* March 6, 1978.

4. See especially *Security Review at Certain NATO Installations,* 121 *Congressional Record* S7184-S7189 (no. 68, April 30, 1975); *First Annual Report to the United States Congress by the Joint Committee on Atomic Energy* (June 30, 1975, Appendix 2, pp. 54-59, Appendix F, pp. 47-51); and the more recent *Hearings* before the Military Installations and Facilities Subcommittee of the House Committee on Armed Services, April 1977.

5. See *Hearings* before the Committee on Governmental Affairs, U.S. Senate, on "An Act To Combat International Terrorism," January 23–March 23, 1978, U.S. Government, Washington D.C., 1978, hereinafter cited as *Hearings.*

6. See *Hearings,* January 23, 1978, p. 20.

7. Comments by David E. McGiffert, assistant secretary of defense for international security affairs, *Hearings,* February 22, 1978, pp. 193-194. The terrorist threat to U.S. nuclear weapons is also recognized by the Department of Defense *Nuclear Weapons Security Primer,* which bears an April 1, 1975, publication date: "International terrorism, during the past few years, has demonstrated that it is a force to be reckoned with. Because of the violent, efficient, and rapid manner by which terrorist acts have been executed, terrorism poses a potential threat to our weapon stockpile and is driving most of the new security upgrade efforts." (Cited in *Development, Use, and Control of Nuclear Energy for the Common Defense and Security and for Peaceful Purposes,* First Annual Report to the United States Congress by the Joint Committee on Atomic Energy, U.S. Government, June 30, 1975, p. 23.)

8. See Department of Defense *Fact Sheet*, "U.S. Military Capabilities for Conducting Counter-Terrorist Operations," *Hearings*, p. 197.

9. See Department of Defense, "U.S. Military Forces With Counter-terrorist Capabilities," *Hearings*, pp. 195-196.

10. See remarks by Senator John Glenn, *Hearings*, March 23, 1978, p. 286.

11. See remarks by Dr. Victor Gilinsky, Commissioner of the Nuclear Regulatory Commission, *Hearings*, March 23, 1978, p. 316.

12. See remarks by Senator Glenn; Thomas J. O'Brien, director for security plans and programs, Department of Defense; and Donald M. Kerr, acting assistant secretary for defense programs, Department of Energy, *Hearings*, March 23, 1978, pp. 319-323.

13. Ibid., p. 319.

14. Ibid.

15. Ibid., p. 321.

16. See Mason Willrich and Theodore Taylor, *Nuclear Theft: Risks and Safeguards* (Cambridge, Mass.: Ballinger, 1974), p. 115; William Epstein, *The Last Chance: Nuclear Proliferation and Arms Control* (New York: The Free Press, 1976); Forrest Frank, "Nuclear Terrorism and the Escalation of International Conflict," paper presented to the Annual Meeting of the Midwest Political Science Association, Chicago, Illinois, May 1, 1976; David Krieger, "Terrorists and Nuclear Technology," *The Bulletin of the Atomic Scientists*, 31, no. 6, June 1975; and Ralph Lapp, "The Ultimate Blackmail," *New York Times Magazine*, February 4, 1973, p. 31.

17. See *Safeguards Systems Concepts for Nuclear Material Transportation*, Final Report by the System Development Corporation for the U.S. Nuclear Regulatory Commission, September 1977, pp. 1-6.

18. See Union of Concerned Scientists letter, by Daniel F. Ford, executive director, 1978, undated, p. 2.

19. *Hearings*, March 22, 1978, p. 260.

20. *Hearings*, March 23, 1978, pp. 323-324.

21. A similar problem of "inventory differences" and "materials unaccounted for" was reported in 1974. (See David Burnham, "Thousands of Pounds of Materials Usable in Nuclear Bombs Unaccounted For," *New York Times*, December 29, 1974, p. 26.) Accounting for nuclear materials is, of course, a difficult process. Since each measurement involves an unavoidable uncertainty, the cumulative effect of several thousand measurements can involve a very large loss.

22. See "U.S. Tells Loss of Bomb-Grade Uranium in '60s," *Chicago Tribune*, August 24, 1977.

23. See "Congress was Misled on Nuclear Thefts, Agency Says," *New York Times*, February 26, 1978, p. 25.

24. *Hearings,* March 23, 1978, pp. 327-329.

25. *Hearings,* pp. 921-923; 968-995.

26. *Hearings,* pp. 250-251.

27. See *Nuclear Theft: Risks and Safeguards,* p. 1.

28. *Hearings,* p. 266.

29. Ibid., p. 267.

30. See *Princeton Alumni Weekly,* October 25, 1976.

31. See "Two Small U.S. Journals Have Printed Articles on Building A-Bombs," *New York Times,* March 11, 1979, p. 21.

32. See "Bomb Class Added to College Catalog," *Denver Post,* October 2, 1977.

33. *Hearings,* March 22, 1978, pp. 275-276.

34. See, for example, *Nuclear Security Personnel for Power Plants: Content and Review Procedures for a Security Training and Qualification Program,* Office of Nuclear Reactor Regulation, U.S. Nuclear Regulatory Commission, July 1978; and *Review and Evaluation of the Nuclear Regulatory Commission Safety Research Program,* a report to the Congress of the United States of America, Advisory Committee on Reactor Safeguards, U.S. Nuclear Regulatory Commission, December 1977.

35. See B. L. Welch, statement before the Joint Committee on Atomic Energy, p. 32.

36. See Robert R. Jones, "Nuclear Reactor Risks—Some Frightening Scenarios," *Chicago Sun-Times,* April 30, 1976. For the improved security regulations, see *Improvements Needed in the Program for the Protection of Special Nuclear Material,* Comptroller General of the United States, General Accounting Office, June 1974.

37. See Jones, *Nuclear Reactor Risks,* p. 12.

38. Ibid.

39. *Hearings,* January 23, 1978, pp. 67-68.

40. See *Report of the Risk Assessment Review Group,* H. W. Lewis, chairman, NUREG/CR-0400, September 1978, p. 45.

41. *Hearings,* pp. 71, 640-654, 244-247.

42. *Hearings,* pp. 246, 640-641.

43. *Hearings,* p. 245.

44. A prominent exception to the terrorist doctrine of indiscriminacy is Carlos Marighella's *Minimanual of the Urban Guerrilla.* According to Marighella, a Brazilian Communist who established the terrorist organization Action for National Liberation (ALN), the urban guerrilla "follows a political goal and only attacks the government, the big capitalists, and the foreign imperialists, particularly North Americans." See Walter Laqueur, ed., *The Guerrilla Reader* (New York: New American Library, 1977), excerpt from the *Minimanual,* p. 219. Similarly, Abraham Guillen, one of

the principal theoreticians of urban guerrilla tactics, argues that the creation of a general climate of terror is both wrong and impolitic: "A popular army that resorts to unnecessary violence, that is not a symbol of justice, equity, liberty, and security, cannot win popular support in the struggle against a dehumanized tyranny." (See Laqueur above, "Urban Guerrilla Strategy," p. 234.)

45. This point is overlooked by most current definitions of terrorism. For example, in the CIA Research Study, *International and Transnational Terrorism: Diagnosis and Prognosis,* April 1976, the common characteristics of international and transnational terrorism are defined as follows: "The threat or use of violence for political purposes when (1) such action is intended to influence the attitudes and behavior of a target group wider than its immediate victims, and (2) its ramifications transcend national boundaries" (p. 1). Abraham Kaplan, of the University of Haifa, says the following: "I mean by terror the use of force primarily to produce a certain fearful state of mind—terror, in fact. Some element of fear is evoked by every exercise of power, in terror, this element looms large, whether as cause or as reason. Moreover, the fear is to be evoked in someone other than those to whom the force is applied. Terror is the use of force in a context that differentiates the *victim* of the violence employed from the *target* of the action, who is to be terrorized." (See "The Psychodynamics of Terrorism," in *Terrorism: An International Journal,* vol. 1, nos. 3 and 4, 1978, p. 239.) According to Baljit Singh, "Terror incorporates two facets: (1) state of fear or anxiety within an individual or a group; and (2) the tool that induces the state of fear. Thus, terror entails the threat or use of symbolic violent acts aimed at influencing political behavior." (See Baljit Singh, "Political Terrorism: An Overview," a paper presented at the thirty-fourth Annual Meeting of the Midwest Political Science Association, May 1976, p. 3.) Charles A. Russell, Leon J. Banker, Jr., and Bowman H. Miller suggest that terrorism involves "the threatened or actual use of force or violence to attain a political goal through fear, coercion, or intimidation." (See "Out-Inventing the Terrorist," mimeograph, Headquarters, Office of Special Investigations, U.S. Air Force, Washington, D.C., May 17, 1977, pp. 2-3.) Two scholars who have produced substantially more useful definitions, however, have been Irving Howe and Burton Leiser. According to Howe, "the one element common to the various kinds of terror is the wish to create unmanageable fear through a use of violence that breaks down traditionally accepted distinctions between combatant and civilian." (See Irving Howe, "The Ultimate Price of Random Terror," *Skeptic,* no. 11, January/February 1976, p. 15.) And Leiser states: "Terrorism is any organized set of acts of violence designed to create an atmosphere of despair or fear, to shake the faith of ordinary citizens in

their government and its representatives, to destroy the structure of authority which normally stands for security, or to reinforce and perpetuate a government regime whose popular support is shaky. It is a policy of seemingly senseless, irrational, and arbitrary murder, assassination, sabotage, subversion, robbery, and other forms of violence, all committed with dedicated indifference to existing legal and moral codes or with claims to special exemption from conventional social norms. The policies of terrorists are pursued with the conviction that the death and suffering of innocent persons who have little or no direct connection with the causes to which the terrorists are dedicated are fully justified by whatever success terrorists may enjoy in achieving their political ends." (See Burton M. Leiser, "Terrorism, Guerrilla Warfare, and International Morality," *Stanford Journal of International Studies,* vol. 12, spring 1977, p. 39.)

46. See Yehoshafat Harkabi, "Al Fatah's Doctrine," in Walter Laqueur, ed., *The Terrorism Reader* (New York: New American Library, 1978), p. 151.

47. Ibid., p. 150.

48. See Mikhail Bakhunin, *Neskolko slov k molodym bratyam v Rossii,* Geneva, 1869, cited by Walter Laqueur, ed., *The Terrorism Reader,* p. 65.

49. See "Again, Death on 'Flight SAM-7'," *Time,* February 26, 1979, p. 40.

50. See G. S. Graber, *The History of the SS* (New York: David McKay Company, 1978), p. 144. See also Lucy S. Dawidowicz, *The War Against the Jews, 1933-1945* (New York: Holt, Rinehart and Winston, 1975), p. 129.

51. See "Urban Guerrilla Strategy," in Walter Laqueur, ed., *The Guerrilla Reader,* p. 233.

52. See Herbert Marcuse, *Counterrevolution and Revolt* (Boston: Beacon Press, 1972), p. 52.

53. See Gerald Priestland, *The Future of Violence* (London: Hamish Hamilton, 1974), p. 155.

54. See Charles A. Russell, et al., "Out-Inventing the Terrorist," reprinted in *Hearings,* p. 832.

55. Ibid.

56. It should be pointed out, however, that there are classical writings on international law that support intervention on humanitarian grounds. For example, Grotius regarded it as a duty of foreign nations to intervene when "a tyrant practices atrocities towards his subjects" (Book 2 of *The Law of War and Peace*). And Pufendorf expressed a similar idea in Book 8 of his *The Law of Nature and Nations.* But the modern international law of human rights, while rejecting an absolute doctrine of freedom from

external interference, does not countenance the support of terrorist violence by certain states against other states.

57. The Soviet Union and East Germany have now allegedly opened special training camps for Palestinians in East Germany, Czechoslovakia, Hungary, South Yemen, and Iraq. See "Palestinian Terrorism: The International Connection," *Backgrounder,* The Heritage Foundation, December 8, 1978, p. 13.

58. See Walter Laqueur, *The Terrorism Reader,* p. 119.

59. See Abstract of Rand Paper, P-5261, "International Terrorism: A New Kind of Warfare," June 1974, 13pp, cited in *A Bibliography of Selected Rand Publications,* January 1977, p. 2.

60. See Brian Jenkins, "International Terrorism: A New Mode of Conflict," Research Paper no. 48, California Seminar on Arms Control and Foreign Policy (Los Angeles: Crescent Publications, 1975), p. 21.

61. See Research Study, *International and Transnational Terrorism: Diagnosis and Prognosis,* CIA, p. 29.

62. See Report by Comdr. R. E. Bigney, USN, et al., Defense Documentation Center, Defense Supply Agency, June 3, 1974, p. 41.

63. See Hersch Lauterpacht, *International Law,* vol. 3., *The Law of Peace,* pts. 2-6 (Cambridge: Cambridge University Press, 1977), p. 274.

Chapter 3

1. See testimony by Dr. Theodore B. Taylor, presented to the Senate Committee on Governmental Affairs, March 22, 1978, *Hearings* on "An Act to Combat International Terrorism," p. 266.

2. See testimony by Dimitri A. Rotow, *Hearings,* March 22, 1978, p. 273.

3. See Mason Willrich and Theodore B. Taylor, *Nuclear Theft: Risks and Safeguards* (Cambridge, Mass.: Ballinger, 1974), p. 22.

4. See U.S. Congress, Office of Technology Assessment, *Nuclear Proliferation and Safeguards* (New York: Praeger, 1977), p. 146.

5. See *Nuclear Theft: Risks and Safeguards,* p. 27.

6. Ibid.

7. See Edmund Faltermayer, "Exorcising the Nightmare of Reactor Meltdowns," *Fortune,* March 12, 1979, p. 82.

8. See *Nuclear Power: Issues and Choices,* Report of the Nuclear Energy Policy Study Group, sponsored by the Ford Foundation, administered by the Mitre Corporation (Cambridge, Mass.: Ballinger, 1977), p. 224. For an interesting early assessment of the Rasmussen Report, see H. A. Bethe, "The Necessity of Fission Power," *Scientific American,* vol. 234, no. 1, January 1976, pp. 21-31.

9. See *Risk Assessment Review Group Report,* U.S. Nuclear Regulatory Commission, H. W. Lewis, chairman, Washington, D.C., September 1978, Bibliographic data sheet.

10. Ibid., p. vi.

11. Ibid.

12. Ibid., pp. viii-x.

13. See Andrei D. Sakharov, *Progress, Coexistence, and Intellectual Freedom* (New York: W. W. Norton, 1968), p. 37.

14. See *Economic and Social Consequences of Nuclear Attacks on the United States,* A study prepared for the Joint Committee on Defense Production, Congress of the United States, published by the Committee on Banking, Housing, and Urban Affairs, United States Senate, U.S. Government Printing Office, Washington, D.C., March 1979, p. v.

15. See Bernard T. Feld, "The Consequences of Nuclear War," *Bulletin of the Atomic Scientists,* vol. 32, no. 6, June 1976, p. 12.

16. See *Economic and Social Consequences of Nuclear Attacks on the United States,* pp. 35-36.

17. Ibid., p. v.

18. See *Long-Term Worldwide Effects of Multiple Nuclear-Weapons Detonations,* Committee to Study the Long-Term Worldwide Effects of Multiple Nuclear-Weapons Detonations, Assembly of Mathematical and Physical Sciences, National Research Council, National Academy of Sciences, Washington, D.C., 1975.

19. *Economic and Social Consequences of Nuclear Attacks on the United States,* p. 2.

20. See *Long-Term Worldwide Effects of Multiple Nuclear-Weapons Detonations,* p. 60.

21. Ibid., p. 66.

22. Ibid., p. 85.

23. Ibid., pp. 12-13.

24. See Tom Stonier, *Nuclear Disaster* (New York: Meridian, 1964), p. 54.

25. See *Economic and Social Consequences of Nuclear Attacks on the United States,* p. 21.

26. See John Willett, ed. and tr., *Brecht on Theatre* (New York: Hill and Wang, 1964), p. 27.

Chapter 4

1. See Robert H. Kupperman, *Facing Tomorrow's Terrorist Incident Today,* U.S. Department of Justice, Law Enforcement Assistance Administration, Washington, D.C., October 1977, p. 5.

2. See *Hearings* before the Committee on Governmental Affairs, U.S. Senate, on "An Act to Combat International Terrorism," testimony of Victor Gilinsky, commissioner of the Nuclear Regulatory Commission, March 23, 1978, p. 316.

3. Ibid.

4. See U.S. Nuclear Regulatory Commission, Office of Management Program and Analysis, *Domestic Safeguards,* Annual Report to the Congress, Fiscal Year 1978, NUREG-0524, Washington, D.C., January 1979, Appendix D, "Future Safeguards Program," pp. D-1-4.

5. See "Safeguards Systems Concepts for Nuclear Material Transportation," Final Report, prepared for the U.S. Nuclear Regulatory Commission, Division of Safeguards, by the System Development Corporation, September 1977, NUREG-0335, NRC-13.

6. See *Hearings,* p. 316.

7. See "Extracts From Nuclear Weapons Security Primer," prepared by the Department of Defense, April 1, 1975, in *First Annual Report to the U.S. Congress by the Joint Committee on Atomic Energy,* June 30, 1975, pp. 83-86.

8. According to Article 6 of the Treaty on the Non-Proliferation of Nuclear Weapons: "Each of the Parties to the Treaty undertakes to pursue negotiations in good faith on effective measures relating to cessation of the nuclear arms race at an early date and to nuclear disarmament, and on a treaty on general and complete disarmament under strict and effective international control."

9. See *Seventeenth Annual Report of the U.S. Arms Control and Disarmament Agency,* U.S. Government, Washington, D.C., May 1978, p. 14.

10. On this point, see Ted Greenwood, et al., *Nuclear Proliferation: Motivations, Capabilities, and Strategies for Control* (New York: McGraw-Hill, 1977), p. 13.

11. See Office of Technology Assessment, *Nuclear Proliferation and Safeguards* (New York: Praeger, 1977), p. 81.

12. See Lewis A. Dunn, "The Role of Sanctions in Non-Proliferation Strategy," Final Report of the Hudson Institute, prepared for the Office of Technology Assessment, U.S. Congress, February 2, 1977, pp. 1-2.

13. See letter by Alys Brody Bohn, *New York Times,* June 4, 1978, p. 18 E.

14. Ibid.

Chapter 5

1. If a terrorist group displaying the self-sacrificing value system of *fedayeen* were also to exhibit traits of ordinary criminality, e.g., bank

robberies ("expropriation") to obtain funds, such traits might assist the efforts of counternuclear terrorist strategists. This is the case because such traits could be publicized widely, undercutting the group's vital bases of popular support.

2. Historically, many violent acts of terrorist groups *have* alienated popular support and *have* been counterproductive to political objectives. As examples, we may point to the acts of the Stern Gang (especially the murder of Lord Moyne in Cairo in 1944, which inspired the Jewish Agency to launch a counterterrorist campaign); the FLQ (especially the killing of French-Canadian Cabinet Minister LaPorte); the Malayan terrorists of the 1950s; the *Organisation de l'Armée Secrète* (OAS) in Algeria; the Turkish People's Liberation Army; the U.S. Weathermen; and the Netherlands' South Moluccan terrorists. It is worth pointing out, however, that the practice of terror and cruelty can occasionally elicit support and admiration as well as revulsion. In writing about the history of bandits, for example, Eric Hobsbawm has indicated that bandits have often become heroes not in spite of their terrible cruelty (cruelty, incidentally, beside which some examples of modern terrorism pale into insignificance), but *because of it*. The hero image stems not from their presumed ability to right wrongs, but to *avenge*. In describing the Colombian *violencia* during the peasant revolution of the years after 1948, Hobsbawm points out that bandits who chopped prisoners into tiny fragments before whole villages and ripped fetuses from pregnant women became instant heroes to the local population. (See Eric Hobsbawm, *Bandits* (New York: Dell, 1969).

What this suggests, from the point of view of effective counternuclear terrorism, is that the ability to convince terrorist groups that higher-order acts of violence are apt to be self-defeating may be impossible in certain contexts. In such cases, where resort to nuclear terrorism may actually generate admiration and support, efforts to prevent this terrorism must center on other bases of deterrence.

3. It is ironic that the mainspring of global security has always been the threat to punish rather than the promise to reward. After all, beginning with studies of child rearing, the literature on behavior modification regularly underscores the idea that positive sanctions are more effective than negative ones, that—speaking metaphorically—we can influence more flies with honey than with vinegar. In reference to reducing the probability of nuclear terrorism, we must begin to look at some carrots as well as the usual sticks.

4. Prior to the advent of concern for higher-order acts of terrorism, the idea that governments would engage in substantive bargaining with terrorists that might lead to major concessions was widely criticized. Today, however, we must face up to the fact that the execution of certain terrorist threats could have genuinely system-destructive effects. Recognizing this,

the hard-line unwillingness to bargain and concede can no longer be regarded as a fixed and irrevocable position of responsible governments. Moreover, a willingness to offer certain concessions to terrorist demands need not be construed as a sign of weakness. Not only does it have the effect of buying time while other courses of action are explored, it is a reversible policy that does not necessarily signal continuing capitulation.

5. Conceptually, it is worth remembering here that violence and power tend to be opposites, and that excessive reliance upon the former signifies an insufficiency of the latter.

6. Some of the problems associated with such a strategy in a world system that is founded upon the principles of realpolitik concern the appearance of "bribes." Even if a strategy of positive sanctions is worked out that looks exceptionally promising, the public reaction to it may be exceedingly unfavorable. Matters of honor and courage, therefore, may mitigate against the operation of positive sanctions in counternuclear terrorist strategies.

Another problem associated with the operation of positive sanctions in such strategies centers on the possibility that some terrorists who display the self-sacrificing value system of *fedayeen* thrive on violent action for its own sake. They are unconcerned with the political object or matters of personal gain. Here, we are clearly up against a brick wall, the reductio ad absurdum of deterrence logic, since the only incentives that might be extended to deter acts of violence are the opportunities to commit such acts.

And then there is the "blackmail" problem. The habitual use of rewards to discourage terrorist violence is apt to encourage terrorists to extort an ever-expanding package of "gifts" in exchange for "good behavior." Here, we must confront the prospect of terrorism as a "protection racket" on a global scale.

7. A variation of this type of terrorist group is one in which the overarching motives are genuinely political, but where ordinary criminality is engaged in to secure needed capital. Here, the primary activity of the group often centers on "expropriation," the long-established euphemism for robberies designed to supply terrorists with funds. The history of this tactic dates back to the Russian expropriators of the 1860s and 1870s. Later, Lenin was careful about maintaining a firm line between expropriations and ordinary crime, but today's expropriators, e.g., the Baader-Meinhof group, Symbionese Liberation Army, and Tupamaros, have expressed far less concern about making a distinction. From the standpoint of effective counterterrorism, such diminished sensitivity is clearly desirable, since it makes it much easier for the government to equate the terrorist robberies with orthodox criminality.

8. This possibility is recognized not only by counterterrorist planners, but by some of the terrorists themselves. For example, in writing about the Uruguayan Tupamaros, Abraham Guillen has written: "The Tupamaros are perilously close to resembling a political Mafia. In demanding large sums of money in ransom for political hostages they have sometimes appeared to be self-serving. It matters little to the average citizen whether bank deposits pass into the hands of 'expropriators' who do little directly to lighten the public burden." ("Urban Guerrilla Strategy" in Walter Laqueur, ed., *The Guerrilla Reader* [New York: New American Library, 1977], p. 237.)

9. In the United States, the example of the Black Panther Party best illustrates the progressive takeover of a militant, political organization by criminal elements. For information on this takeover, see especially *Gun-Barrel Politics, The Black Panther Party*, 1966-1971, Report by the Committee on Internal Security, House of Representatives, Washington, D.C., August 18, 1971.

10. See, for example, Ted Robert Gurr, *Why Men Rebel* (Princeton: Princeton University Press, 1970), especially pp. 241-242, 259, and 274; Arnold H. Buss, *The Psychology of Aggression* (New York: Wiley, 1961), p. 58; and Leonard Berkowitz, *Aggression: A Social Psychological Analysis* (New York: McGraw-Hill, 1962), p. 96.

11. If a terrorist group with such characteristics were also to exhibit traits of expropriatory criminality, the deterrence effort might also exploit the negative public opinion associated with these traits.

12. In this connection, governments must avoid the impression that the prospective costs of nuclear violence are so great as to warrant any and all concessions. Rather, prior to the onset of an actual incident, governments should create a hierarchy of concessions, ranging from the most easily satisfied financial demands to the most sweeping transformations of government policy and personnel. With such a hierarchy in hand, responsible officials could at least enter into a protracted bargaining situation with prospective nuclear terrorists, pursuing a concessionary policy that is both incremental and consistent with predetermined calculations of tolerable losses. Moreover, such preincident planning might also allow the government to take the offensive position in the bargaining situation.

13. For an example of the efficacy of threats of mild punishment, we may consider the concessions that were made to the Hanafi Moslems who held captive three Washington buildings and 149 hostages in March 1977. These concessions centered on releasing terrorists on bond at the close of the incident.

14. Terrorists have long understood that harsh and repressive countermeasures often work in their own interests. With such an understanding,

they have even developed tactics designed to goad governments into over-reaction. In Algeria, FLN strategy was designed to provoke the kind of countermeasures that would make compromise impossible. More recently, the IRA and the Tupamaros have deliberately prodded government repression in an attempt to alienate moderates' support of the government and erode faith in the political system. From the standpoint of effective counternuclear terrorism strategies, these points suggest that governments give careful scrutiny to the prospective costs of harsh physical countermeasures before implementing such measures. Contrary to the facile conventional wisdom on the subject, fighting fire with fire is not always effective. Sometimes, it is much better to rely on water.

15. See Hannah Arendt, *On Violence* (New York: Harcourt, Brace, and World, 1970), p. 56.

16. Despite the revulsion that is typically generated by the suggestion of assassination in liberal, democratic societies, there is a well-established tradition in political philosophy that regards it as permissible under certain circumstances, e.g., the writings of Cicero, St. Thomas Aquinas, and Sir Thomas More.

17. To a certain extent, the different ways in which governments currently balance their commitments to safety and civil liberties are revealed by their different legal conditions. For example, the antiterrorist laws in Germany, France, England, and Sweden reflect different kinds of cost-benefit calculations.

Organizational crimes, or conspiracy, are punishable in the Federal Republic of Germany (FRG), France, and England, but not in Sweden.

In reference to grounds for arrest, the West German Criminal Procedure Code stipulates that "urgent suspicion" is sufficient for members of a terrorist association. French law identifies the "endangerment of public safety" as adequate grounds. English law leaves the matter entirely to the Court's evaluation of the case made by the prosecuting authorities. And the Swedish solution is very similar to that of the FRG.

The legal situation in the United States is not governed by specific antiterrorist legislation. But important points of comparison do exist. The notion of criminal conspiracy is well-defined under U.S. law, but it requires the commission of an overt act—a requirement not present in the West German, English, and French systems. Similarly, the grounds for arrest are generally more stringent than in the other national systems being compared, even when the arrest is based upon a judgment of "probable cause" rather than a magistrate's warrant. Finally, only minor restrictions are imposed concerning the prevention of contact between the defense attorney and the defendant, a situation markedly more liberal than that of West Germany and substantially more liberal than in France and England.

These points are taken from a comparative survey of the main anti-terrorist laws in West Germany, France, England, and Sweden published in the December 5, 1977, issue of the West German newsmagazine *Der Spiegel,* and a translation of this survey by Ronald F. Storette and Axel Heck, prepared for the German Information Center, Federal Republic of Germany. It should be noted that at the time of this writing, an anti-terrorist bill sponsored by Senators Ribicoff and Javits, S. 333, has been introduced in the U.S. Congress. This act is cited as the "Omnibus Anti-terrorism Act of 1979."

18. Similarly, goaded by the kidnapping of former Premier Aldo Moro in March 1978, Italian authorities declared a "situation of emergency" and ordered broadened police powers to cope with the threat. These powers included greater discretion in wiretapping and authorization to question suspects immediately without a lawyer being present.

19. It should not be assumed, however, that strategies of counter-nuclear terrorism that severely infringe civil liberties would necessarily be effective. The adoption of severe measures to curtail terrorism could impair civil liberties without providing any counterterrorist benefits. Indeed, such measures might even incite the very terrorist excesses they are designed to prevent.

20. Under international law, however, the range of protection granted to participants in noninternational armed conflicts is quite limited. Although the prisoners taken in such conflicts must be treated in accordance with general principles of humanity, they cannot claim the privilege of prisoners of war. Rather, they may be treated as criminals under municipal law. The core of international legal protection for participants in internal wars is Article 3, common to the four Geneva Conventions of August 12, 1949.

21. However, even when survival itself is at stake, decent governments must resist descending to counterterrorist policies of "prophylaxis" as they are practiced in the Soviet Union and other authoritarian societies. Such policies, having their historical roots in the arbitrary arrest provisions of the Law of 1793 during the French Reign of Terror, represent so great an assault on fundamental human rights that they destroy the very values that counterterrorism is designed to protect.

22. Although every act of terrorism is clearly "criminal" insofar as it violates certain laws in the criminal codes of particular jurisdictions, in the decision-making taxonomy the term "criminal" is applied only where robbery is adopted to secure funds. Moreover, as it is used in the taxonomy, the term "criminal" refers to behavior that does not qualify as a "political crime" under international law.

23. This obligation is conferred upon states by Article 2(4) of the UN

charter. A similar obligation was imposed by Article 10 of the League covenant. The principle was reaffirmed by the International Court of Justice in 1949 in the Corfu Channel Case.

24. Where such action is taken, and prisoners taken, their status would not necessarily be the privileged one of lawful combatants. Under the Geneva Convention of 1949, which reaffirms earlier principles of the Hague Regulations of 1899 and 1907, four requirements must be met to qualify for treatment as a prisoner of war: (1) be commanded by a person responsible for his subordinates; (2) have a fixed distinctive sign recognizable at a distance; (3) carry arms openly; and (4) conduct operations in accordance with the laws and customs of war. Where these requirements are not met, the terrorist prisoners would not be due the benefits of privileged treatment.

25. In terms of international law, support for such sanctions can be found as far back as the eighteenth century in Emmerich de Vattel's *The Law of Nations.* According to Vattel, "If there should be found a restless and unprincipled nation, ever ready to do harm to others, to thwart their purposes, and to stir up civil strife among their citizens, there is no doubt that all others would have the right to unite together to subdue such a nation, to discipline it, and even to disable it from doing further harm."

26. See Friedlander, "Terrorism and International Law: What is Being Done," *Rutgers Camden Law Journal,* vol. 8, no. 3, spring 1977, p. 386.

27. One recent attempt is built into the Final Document of the Conference on Terrorism and Political Crimes, June 4-16, 1972, Syracuse, Italy. According to Article 6 of this document:

1. The proposal to create such a court reaffirms a lengthy history on the subject, support for which has been expressed by distinguished jurists since the end of World War I, and was manifested in the 1937 Convention on the Prevention and Punishment of Terrorism and the two draft conventions elaborated by United Nations Committees in 1951 and 1953.
2. It is recommended once again that such a court be established with jurisdiction over international crimes and in particular over acts falling within the definition of terrorism.
3. A draft statute for such a court should be elaborated at the earliest opportunity, taking into consideration several existing proposals and in particular the proposed 1953 United Nations draft. Such a statute should also include questions of enforcement and sanctions.
4. The court should exercise its jurisdiction over persons and corporate entities but not over states, since questions involving states are within the jurisdiction of the International Court of Justice.
5. The proposed International Criminal Court could be created by the United Nations or be an organ thereof, as in the case of the International Court of Justice, or be independently created and operated as an autonomous international body. The realization of such a proposal could be by virtue of:

   a. a single multilateral treaty-statute;
   b. multilateral treaties on this and other subjects;
   c. bilateral treaties;
   d. amending protocols to existing international conventions;
   e. unilateral declarations;
   f. enactment of national legislation; or,
   g. voluntary submission to the jurisdiction of such Court or any other special arrangement.

(See M. Cherif Bassiouni, *International Terrorism and Political Crimes* [Springfield, Ill.: C. C. Thomas, 1975], pp. xviii-xix.)

28. This standard has roots in the earlier decisions of other national courts that define the principle that terrorism must be excluded from the realm of political crimes on matters concerning extradition. A particularly important case in this regard is the decision of a Swiss court in the *Pavan Case* of 1928. Here, the court ruled that the political-offense exemption for extradition did not obtain because there was no *direct link* between the act of terrorism (the killing by an Italian of a fascist intelligence agent in France) and the destruction of the Italian regime.

29. See John Dugard, "International Terrorism and the Just War," *The Stanford Journal of International Studies*, vol. 12, spring 1977, p. 32.

30. See GAOR, 27th Session, 6th Committee (UN Doc. A/C.6/SR. 1368, 54, Nov. 21, 1972; cited by Dugard, "International Terrorism," p. 33.

31. See "Serbian Court Refuses to Extradite Four Sought by Bonn in Terrorism," *New York Times*, November 19, 1978, p. 23.

32. See M. Cherif Bassiouni, ed., *International Terrorism and Political Crimes,* (Springfield, Illinois: Charles C. Thomas, 1975), pp. xix-xx.

33. Ibid., p. xii.

34. See John Dugard, "International Terrorism," pp. 21-37.

35. It should be noted that concern for these principles is an integral part of the laws of war of international law.

36. See Elie Wiesel, *A Jew Today* (New York: Random House, 1978), p. 94.

37. Ibid., p. 95.

Chapter 6

1. The connection seems to be understood in a special light by Herbert Marcuse. Although not speaking about international politics directly, Marcuse recognizes the paradoxical and self-defeating efforts of "society" to impose principles of nonviolence on the opposition while systematically enlarging its arena of "legitimate" violence. Understood in terms of the problem of nuclear terrorism, the philosopher's wisdom sug-

gests a clear nexus between the state's characteristic mode of security seeking and the penchant for terrorist violence. See Herbert Marcuse, *Counterrevolution and Revolt* (Boston: Beacon Press, 1972), p. 52.

2. See William Irwin Thompson, *Passages About Earth: An Exploration of the New Planetary Culture* (New York: Harper and Row, 1974), pp. 131-132.

3. See Jonas Salk, *The Survival of the Wisest* (New York: Harper and Row, 1973), p. 82.

4. From the standpoint of post–World War II history, there has been a stready shift from an initial era of bipolarity to one of multipolarity. The actual time of the transfer, however, is a matter of continuing disagreement among statesmen and scholars. Former President Nixon identified the shift away from bipolarity as a phenomenon of the 1970s (see Nixon, "United States Foreign Policy for the 1970s: The Emerging Structure of Peace," a report to the Congress, February 9, 1972); John Herz speaks of the passing of bipolarity in the late 1950s (see Herz, *International Politics in the Atomic Age* [New York: Columbia University Press, 1962], p. 34); Zbigniew Brzezinski notes that the decline of bipolarity was completed by 1968 (see Brzezinski, "How The Cold War Was Played," *Foreign Affairs* 51, October 1972, p. 207); Michael J. Brenner reinforces the Nixon view of a contemporary shift (see Brenner, "The Problem of Innovation and the Nixon-Kissinger Foreign Policy," *International Studies Quarterly* 17, September 1973, pp. 255-294); and Kenneth Waltz predicts the continuation of bipolarity until the end of the century (see Waltz, "The Stability of a Bipolar World," *Daedalus* 93, summer 1964, pp. 898-899).

5. While the balance of power appears to have offered two relatively peaceful periods in history, the ones beginning with the Peace of Westphalia and the Congress of Vienna, the hundred-year interval between the Napoleonic wars and the First World War was actually a period of frequent wars in Europe. The fact that the balance of power has been disastrously ineffective in producing peace during our own century hardly warrants mention.

6. Contrariwise, it has been argued persuasively that equilibrium heightens the danger of war by giving all parties the impression of possible victory, whereas disequilibrium deters the weaker sides while the stronger ones lack incentive. For the best examples of this position, see A.F.K. Organski, *World Politics* (New York, Knopf, 1958), p. 292; and John H. Herz, *International Politics in the Atomic Age* (New York: Columbia University Press, 1959), pp. 316-338.

7. This is because there is nothing about the new balance system that is able to ensure the credibility of particular deterrence postures. In its mistaken orientation to notions of selective equilibrium and the prevention of hegemony, multipolarism thus ignores the truly essential basis of peaceful international relations in a world system that lacks government.

It goes almost without saying that multipolarism also ignores a number of other grievously dangerous risks to security, some of which are unrelated to the "deadly logic" of deterrence. These risks are in the form of accidental nuclear war, nuclear war that is precipitated by unauthorized individuals and nuclear war which results from incorrect calculations concerning reciprocity.

8. See Wolfram F. Hanrieder, "The International System: Bipolar or Multibloc," *The Journal of Conflict Resolution*, vol. 9, September 1965, pp. 299-308.

9. Historically, of course, a balance of power system was ushered in with the Peace of Westphalia in 1648, and has been with us ever since. The basic dynamics of this system were reaffirmed at the Peace of Utrecht in 1713; the Congress of Vienna in 1815; and the two world war settlements. Strictly speaking, neither the League of Nations nor the United Nations can qualify as a system of collective security. Rather, both are examples of international organization functioning within a balance of power world. As for world government, even the case of Imperial Rome does not, strictly speaking, fulfill the appropriate criteria, since the extent of its jurisdiction was coextensive with only a portion of the entire world.

10. Among the most widely known exponents of this idea in the history of Western political thought are the following: Dante, *De Monarchia*; Georg Podebrad's planned federation of Christian princes; Pope Leo's proposal; Francois de la Noue, *Discours politiques et militaries*; Emeric Crucé, *Nouveau Cyneé*; Sully, *Le Grand Dessein*; William Penn, *An Essay Towards The Present and Future Peace of Europe by the Establishment of an European Diet, Parliament, or Estates*; John Bellers, *Some Reasons for a European State Proposed to the Powers of Europe*; C. I. Castel de Saint-Pierre, *Projet de paix perpetuelle*; Jean Jacques Rousseau, *A Lasting Peace Through the Federation of Europe*; Jeremy Bentham, *Plan for an Universal and Perpetual Peace*; Immanuel Kant, *Zum ewigen Frieden*.

A vast literature advancing the case for world centralization has its origins in our own century. Among the most notable are the following: Raymond L. Bridgman, *World Organization* (1905); H. G. Wells, *The Common Sense of World Peace* (1929); Clarence K. Streit, *For Union Now* (1939); W. B. Curry, *The Case for a Federal Union* (1939); David Hoadley Munroe, *Hang Together: The Union Now Primer* (1940); Grenville Clark, *A Memorandum With Regard to a New Effort to Organize Peace* (1939); Duncan and Elizabeth Wilson, *Federation and World Order* (1939); Oscar Newfang, *World Government* (1942); Emery Reves, *Anatomy of Peace* (1945); Norman Cousins, *Modern Man is Obsolete* (1945); Cord Meyer, *Peace or Anarchy* (1947); Crane Brinton, *From Many One* (1948); Vernon Nash, *The World Must Be Governed* (1949); Grenville Clark and Louis B. Sohn, *World Peace Through World Law* (1966); Richard A. Falk,

A Study of Future Worlds (1975); and Saul H. Mendlovitz, *On The Creation of a Just World Order* (1975).

11. The distinguished psychiatrist, Jerome D. Frank, has pointed out, "At least seventy-five chiefs of state in the last four centuries led their countries while suffering from severe mental disturbances." See Frank, *Sanity and Survival, Psychological Aspects of War and Peace* (New York: Random House, 1967), p. 59.

12. May 22, 1977, p. 2.

Index